CW01621785

For Mental Arithmetic practice, it has to be CGP!

There's no better way to improve Mental Arithmetic skills than with practice, and this incredible CGP Question Book is packed with the best practice around.

There are stacks of questions tailored to Year 5 pupils, plus Listening Tests with online audio to help develop their listening skills. We've also added regular Progress Tests to keep track of how pupils are doing.

And of course, the answers to every question are available online. You're welcome!

What CGP is all about

Our sole aim here at CGP is to produce the highest quality books — carefully written, immaculately presented and dangerously close to being funny.

Then we work our socks off to get them out to you — at the cheapest possible prices.

Contents

Online Extras

The answers to every question in the book are available online — to find them, scan the QR code on the left with your smartphone or go to cgpbooks.co.uk/MA-Year5.

You'll find links to all of the audio files for the Listening Tests there, too — amazing!

Published by CGP

Editors: Martha Bozic, Abigail Brindley, Michael Bushell, Sarah George, Ruth Greenhalgh, Sean McParland and David Ryan.

With thanks to Alison Griffin and Alison Palin for the proofreading.

With thanks to Jade Sim for the copyright research.

ISBN: 978 1 83774 043 7

Printed by Elanders Ltd, Newcastle upon Tyne.
Clipart from Corel®

Based on the classic CGP style created by Richard Parsons.

About this Book

This book is split into **three sections**. Each section contains mixed tests covering a range of Year 5 Maths topics. You should aim to do all your working **in your head**, without writing anything down.

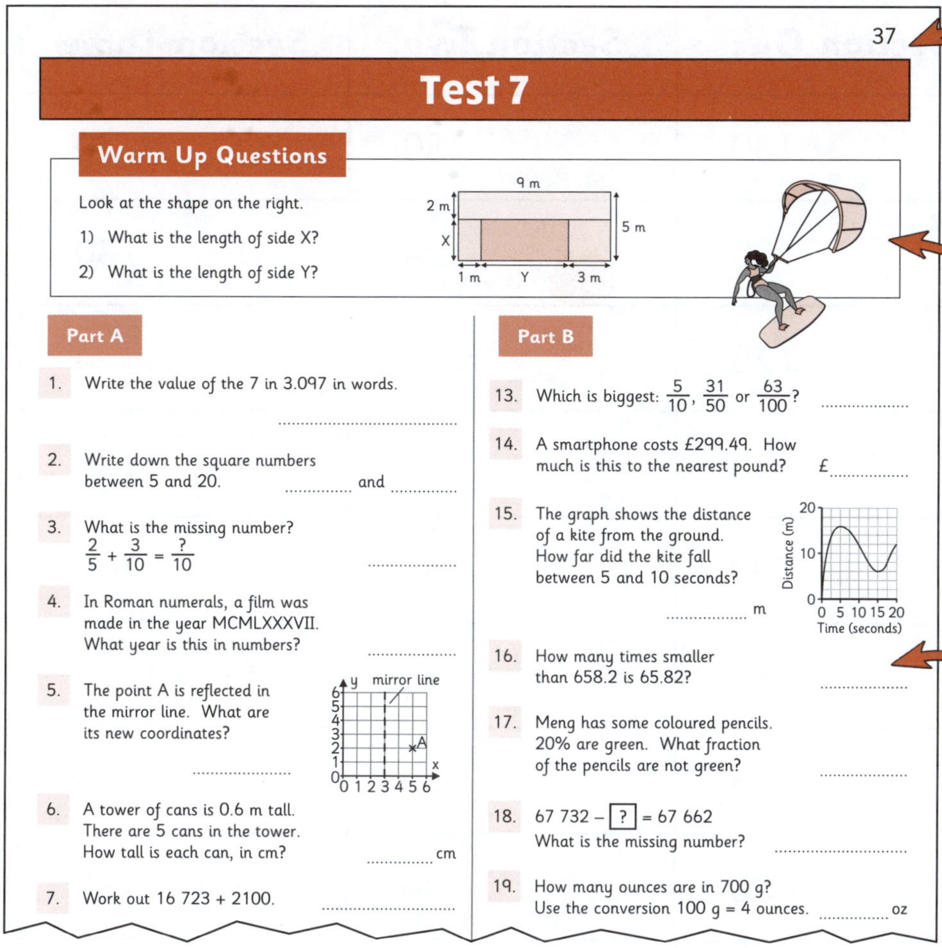
37

Test 7

Warm Up Questions

Look at the shape on the right.

1) What is the length of side X?

2) What is the length of side Y?

Part A

1. Write the value of the 7 in 3.097 in words. ....
2. Write down the square numbers between 5 and 20. .... and ....
3. What is the missing number? $\frac{2}{5} + \frac{3}{10} = \frac{?}{10}$ ....
4. In Roman numerals, a film was made in the year MCMLXXXVII. What year is this in numbers? ....
5. The point A is reflected in the mirror line. What are its new coordinates? ....
6. A tower of cans is 0.6 m tall. There are 5 cans in the tower. How tall is each can, in cm? .... cm
7. Work out 16 723 + 2100. ....

Part B

13. Which is biggest: $\frac{5}{10}$, $\frac{31}{50}$ or $\frac{63}{100}$? ....
14. A smartphone costs £299.49. How much is this to the nearest pound? £....................
15. The graph shows the distance of a kite from the ground. How far did the kite fall between 5 and 10 seconds? .... m
16. How many times smaller than 658.2 is 65.82? ....
17. Meng has some coloured pencils. 20% are green. What fraction of the pencils are not green? ....
18. 67 732 – [?] = 67 662 What is the missing number? ....
19. How many ounces are in 700 g? Use the conversion 100 g = 4 ounces. .... oz

The tests get **trickier** between the sections — the Section 1 tests are easier and the Section 3 tests are a bit harder.

Some tests have **Warm Up Questions** to help get your brain in gear, before you tackle the rest of the questions.

Each test is in **two parts**, so you don't have to do all the questions in the test at once.

There is also a **Progress Test** and three **Listening Tests** at the end of each section. These are the same level of difficulty as the rest of the tests in that section.

The **Progress Tests** cover a range of topics, so you can see how you're getting on with the maths you've seen so far.

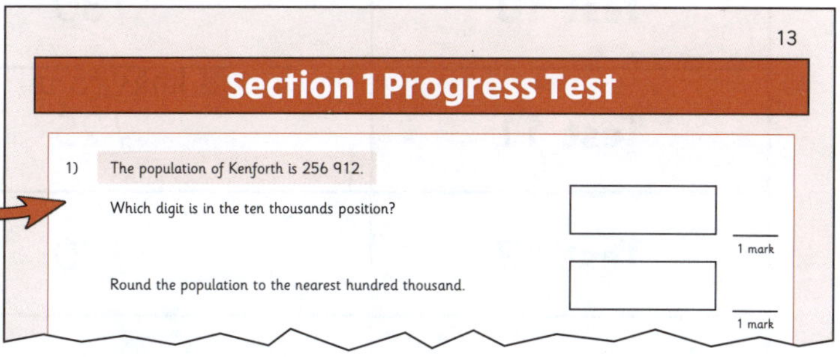
13

Section 1 Progress Test

1) The population of Kenforth is 256 912.

Which digit is in the ten thousands position? 1 mark

Round the population to the nearest hundred thousand. 1 mark

You can find the audio for the **Listening Tests** by either going to cgpbooks.co.uk/MA-Year5 or by scanning the QR code at the top of each Listening Test page.

You will hear each question twice, and then you will have 5 or 10 seconds to answer it.

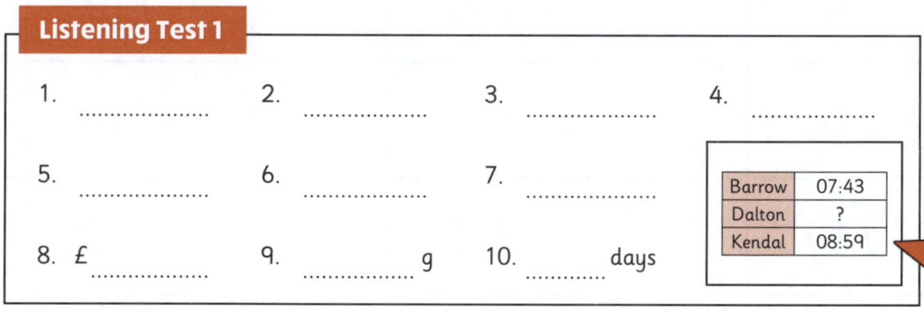
Listening Test 1

1. .... 2. .... 3. .... 4. ....

5. .... 6. .... 7. .... 8. £ ....

9. .... g 10. .... days

Barrow	07:43
Dalton	?
Kendal	08:59

Each Listening Test has one question that uses a **diagram**. You'll find the diagram in the corner of the answer box.

Progress Chart

Use this chart to keep track of your scores in each test.

	Section One	Section Two	Section Three
Test 1	/30	/30	/30
Test 2	/30	/24	/30
Test 3	/25	/30	/24
Test 4	/30	/30	/30
Test 5	/30	/30	/30
Test 6	/30	/24	/30
Test 7	/25	/30	/24
Test 8	/30	/30	/30
Test 9	/30	/30	/30
Test 10	/30	/24	/24
Test 11	/25	/30	/30
Test 12	/30	/30	
Progress Test	/17	/15	/16
Listening Test 1	/10	/10	/10
Listening Test 2	/10	/10	/10
Listening Test 3	/10	/10	/10

Test 1

Part A

1. Which digit is in the thousands position of 18 592? ....

2. A bucket holds 5200 ml of water. How much can it hold in litres? .... litres

3. Which of these numbers is the biggest?
11.28 11.42 11.31 ....

4. What is 19 × 1000? ....

5. 34 530 people live in a town. 100 people move away. How many people now live in the town? ....

6. What is the area of this shape?

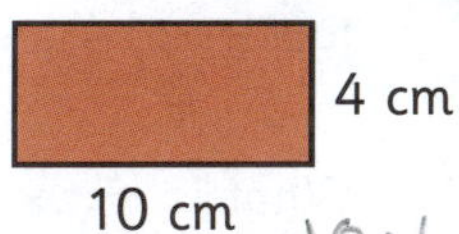

.... cm^2

7. What is the missing number?
235 000 + [?] = 285 000 ....

8. 740 pupils are divided equally into ten groups. How many pupils are in each group? ....

9. A bungalow is 3.7 m high. How high is this in cm? .... cm

10. What is the missing number?
6000 × [?] = 42 000 ....

11. Which pair of numbers is not a factor pair of 24?
[3 and 8] [4 and 7] [2 and 12] ....

12. What is the missing number?

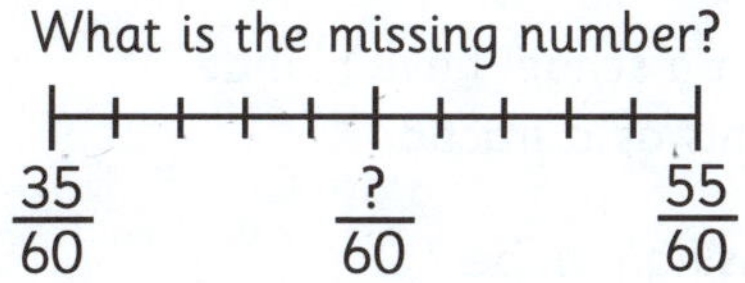

....

13. Start at 34 887 and count backwards 3 steps of 1000. What number do you get? ....

14. Find the missing number.
$23\% = \frac{?}{100}$ ....

15. What is 1.8 rounded to the nearest whole number? ....

Part B

16. It takes a boat 2 hours to sail 10 km. How far can it sail in 24 hours? .... km

17. Use the diagram to work out the missing number in these equivalent fractions.

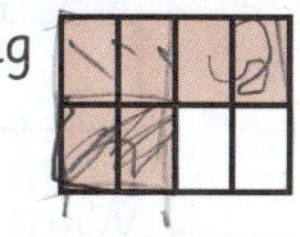

$\frac{6}{8} = \frac{?}{4}$ ....

18. Write 0.89 as a fraction. ....

19. Dennis took one and three-quarter minutes to run around a track. How many seconds did he take? .... s

20. What is the size of angle j?

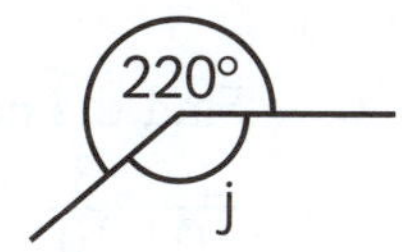

.... °

21. Townsend has a population of 236 679. What is the population rounded to the nearest hundred thousand? ....

22. What number do you get when you count forwards 3 from –7? ....

23. What is 1440 ÷ 12? ....

24. Jade's garden is square and has a perimeter of 32 m. What is the length of one side of the garden? .... m

25. What is 6200 + 1400? ....

26. Ken eats $\frac{1}{8}$ of a box of cereal each day. What fraction does he eat in 3 days? ....

27. Write the first three multiples of 100. ....

28. There are 36 marks in total on a test. Shiva scored 7 out of every 12 marks. How many marks did she score out of 36? ....

29. What is 12 × 15? ....

30. The table shows what type of pie 30 people prefer. How many people prefer cherry pie?

Type of pie	Number of people
Custard	14
Pumpkin	5
Cherry	?

....

Test 2

Part A

1. What is 20 × 100? ....

2. Which number in the box is a multiple of 6?

15	18	22	26

....

3. What is 7.1 rounded to the nearest whole number? ....

4. It is 8 °C in London. It is 10 °C colder in Glasgow. What is the temperature in Glasgow? .... °C

5. What is 3600 – 800? ....

6. Find the next term in this sequence: $\frac{1}{10}, \frac{3}{10}, \frac{5}{10}, \boxed{?}, \ldots$ ....

7. What is 9000 ÷ 1000? ....

8. Which digit is in the millions position of 5 763 409? ....

9. Walnuts cost £0.50 per 200 g. How much does 800 g cost? £..................

10. Find the missing number. $0.3 = \frac{?}{10}$ ....

11. The perimeter of a field is 700 m. Sian runs 5 laps around the field. How far does she run in total? .... m

12. Each cube has a volume of 1 cm³. What is the volume of this cuboid?

.... cm³

13. A cat weighs 4.6 kg. How much does it weigh in g? .... g

14. What is the missing number in these equivalent fractions? Use the diagram to help you.

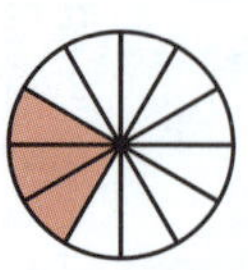

$\frac{3}{12} = \frac{?}{4}$ ....

15. Nasir scored 12 500 points on Level 1 of a game and 3100 points on Level 2. How many points did he score in total? ....

16. Round 188 413 to the nearest ten thousand. ....

Part B

17. Start at 465 160 and count forwards 1 step of 100 000. What number do you get? ....

18. Look at this bus timetable. How long does it take to travel from Nelson Road to Main Street?

Nelson Road	08:15
Oak Square	08:31
Main Street	08:48

.... mins

19. A rectangle is 7 cm long and 4 cm high. What is its area? .... cm²

20. What are the common factors of 4 and 6? .... and ....

21. What is $\frac{3}{10} \times 3$?

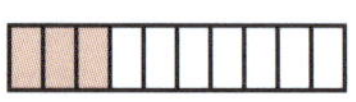

Use the diagram to help you. ....

22. What is the missing number? $17\,900 - \boxed{?} = 14\,900$ ....

23. In an aquarium, 126 fish are shared equally between 3 tanks. How many fish are there in each tank? ....

24. What is the size of angle p? .... °

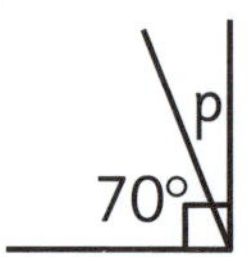

25. Which symbol (< or >) goes in the box? $3.75 \ \boxed{?} \ 3.59$ ....

26. It took Lena 2 minutes 30 seconds to do a puzzle. It took Gary twice as long. How many minutes did it take Gary? .... mins

27. 37% of pupils in a school have blonde hair. What is this as a fraction? ....

28. What is the missing number? $5600 \div \boxed{?} = 700$ ....

29. What is the perimeter of this shape?

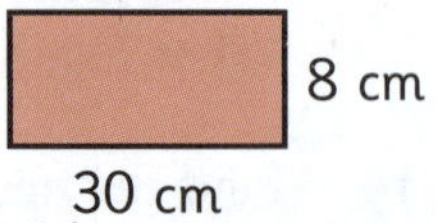

.... cm

30. Lee feeds his hamster 9 pieces of carrot every day. Lee has 180 pieces of carrot. How many days can he feed the hamster for? .... days

Test 3

Warm Up Questions

Look at the bottles on the right.

1) How much more does bottle B contain than bottle A, in litres?

2) How much do the bottles contain in total, in litres?

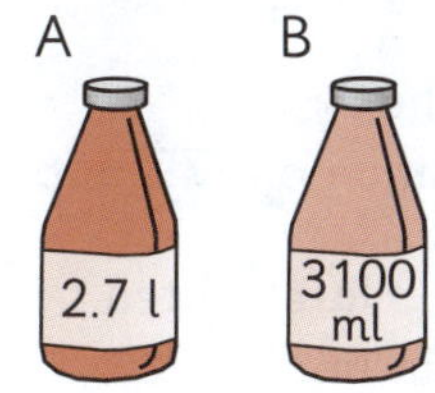

Part A

1. Which of these numbers is the smallest?
4.54 5.21 4.45 ....

2. A rabbit weighs 1500 g.
How much does it weigh in kg? .... kg

3. What is 71% as a decimal? ....

4. What is the area of this shape?
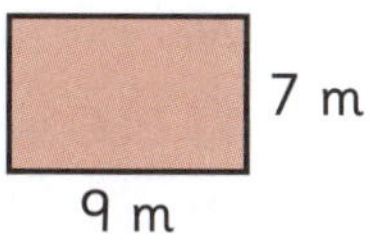

.... m^2

5. What is the missing number?
9 × [?] = 1800 ....

6. Start at –2 and count back 8.
What number do you get? ....

7. 240 pupils are split into teams of 8 for sports day.
How many teams are there? ....

8. What is 14 450 + 10 300? ....

9. What is the missing number?
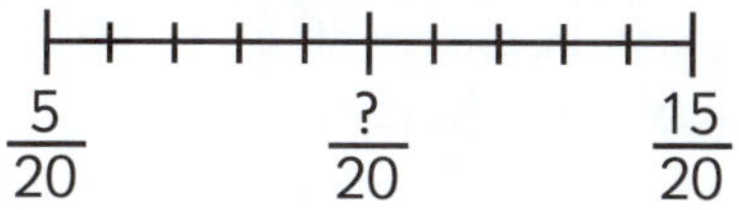

....

10. Which digit is in the ten thousands position of 91 354? ....

11. Katya knits $\frac{2}{5}$ of a scarf each week. How much of the scarf will she knit in 2 weeks? ....

12. What is 44 × 6? ....

13. A rectangle is 30 m long and 15 m wide. What is its perimeter? .... m

Part B

14. What is 1200 + 340? ....

15. A website sells 7 books every minute.
How many does it sell in an hour? ....

16. What is 490 ÷ 1000? ....

17. Which number in the box is a common factor of 16 and 20?

5	8	6	4

....

18. Start at 21 427 and count up 5 steps of 10. What number do you get? ....

19. What is the size of angle d?
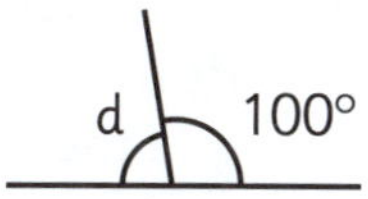

.... °

20. What is the missing number?
12 700 – [?] = 8700 ....

21. Write 0.11 as a fraction. ....

22. What is 3.5 rounded to the nearest whole number? ....

23. What is 2918 × 10? ....

24. The table shows how many frogs some pupils spotted in a pond. How many more frogs did Layla spot than Henry and Taylor combined?

	Number of frogs
Henry	13
Taylor	9
Layla	24

....

25. What is the missing number in these equivalent fractions? Use the diagram to help you.
$\frac{10}{16} = \frac{?}{8}$ ....
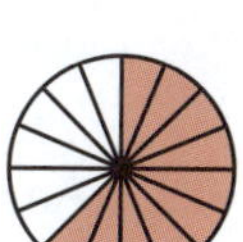

Test 4

Part A

1. Which digit is in the ten thousands position of 372 516? ....

2. A mug contains 0.3 litres of tea. How much is this in ml? .... ml

3. Start at 45 666 and count up 3 steps of 100. What number do you get? ....

4. Which of these is the best estimate for angle a: 45°, 105° or 190°?

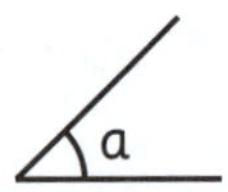

.... °

5. Write the first three multiples of 12. ....

6. What is the missing number?
$0.52 = \frac{?}{100}$ ....

7. What is 10.4 rounded to the nearest whole number? ....

8. What is 6306 ÷ 100? ....

9. Each cube has a volume of 1 cm^3. How many more cubes are needed to give the shape a volume of 24 cm^3?

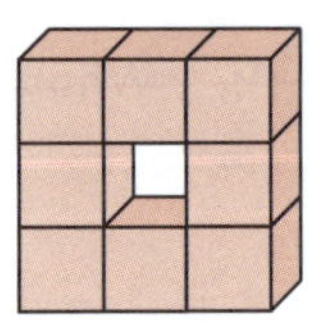

....

10. 2 and what other number make a factor pair of 28? ....

11. Carl has 24 pens. Liz has 4 times as many pens as Carl. How many pens does Liz have? ....

12. What is the missing number?
4 × [?] = 320 ....

13. It is –10 °C in Reykjavik. It is 5 °C warmer in Oslo. What is the temperature in Oslo? .... °C

14. What is 1320 ÷ 11? ....

15. Use the diagram to work out how many fifths are equivalent to $\frac{12}{15}$. ....

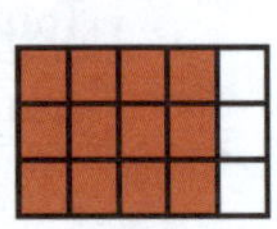

16. Amir thinks of a number. He adds 3500 to it and gets 76 500. What was his original number? ....

Part B

17. What is the perimeter of this shape in cm?

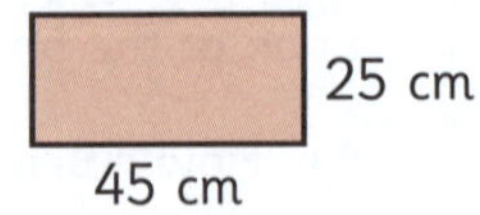

.... cm

18. What is the missing number?
1500 ÷ [?] = 500 ....

19. A pack of gum contains 24 pieces. Helena buys 7 packs. How many pieces of gum does she have in total? ....

20. What is $\frac{1}{6} \times 5$?
Use the diagram to help you.

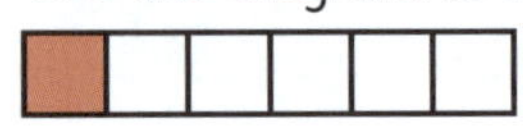

....

21. What is the missing number?
11 500 + [?] = 17 700 ....

22. Eva stayed with her uncle in Peru for 49 days. How long is this in weeks? .... weeks

23. What is the next term in this sequence?
$\frac{3}{24}$, $\frac{6}{24}$, $\frac{9}{24}$, [?], ...

24. There are 2400 ants in an ant farm. 250 escape. How many ants are left? ....

25. What is 46 × 1000? ....

26. There are 72 189 houses in a town. What is this to the nearest thousand? ....

27. 3% of people on a train are reading a book. What is this as a fraction? ....

28. A square tile has an area of 64 cm^2. What is the length of one side? .... cm

29. Which symbol (< or >) should go in the box?
8.91 [?] 8.95 ....

30. Look at this bus timetable. How long does it take to travel from Thatchingham to Pinkbury?

Newburton	13:10
Thatchingham	13:16
Pinkbury	13:36

.... mins

Test 5

Part A

1. Which symbol (< or >) should go in the box?
973 512 [?] 973 489 ....

2. What is 5122 × 10? ....

3. What temperature is 10 °C warmer than –3 °C? .... °C

4. What is 249 525 + 60 000? ....

5. What is the missing number?
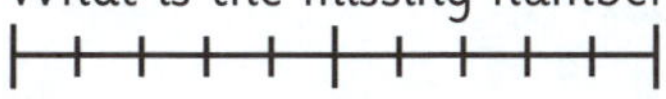
$\frac{20}{80}$ $\frac{?}{80}$ $\frac{70}{80}$ ....

6. A trailer can hold 900 potatoes. How many potatoes fit into 7 trailers? ....

7. What are the only common factors of 7 and 14? .... and ....

8. Jessie has 24 beads on her bracelet. Niall has half as many. How many beads does Niall have on his bracelet? ....

9. Elaine cycles 6.7 km. How far is this in m? .... m

10. What is $\frac{2}{7} \times 2$?
Use the diagram to help you.
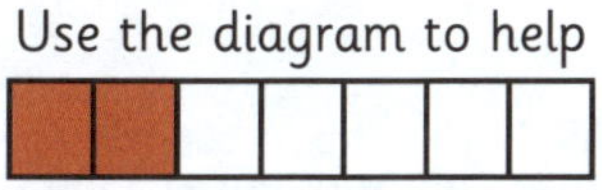
....

11. Which of these numbers is the biggest?
52.61 52.06 52.60 ....

12. Akbar is making bunches of 5 flowers. How many flowers does he need to make 29 bunches? ....

13. Find the missing number.
$0.9 = \frac{?}{10}$ ....

14. The table shows what colour 45 people prefer. How many people prefer blue?

Colour	Number of people
Pink	15
Blue	?
Red	18

....

15. A hamster weighs 150 g. What is this in kg? .... kg

Part B

16. A square has side lengths of 3 cm. What is its area? .... cm^2

17. What is 1951 ÷ 100? ....

18. What is 17.4 rounded to the nearest whole number? ....

19. What is the perimeter of this rectangle? .... cm
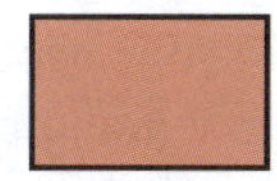

20. A warehouse shares 312 crates equally between 6 lorries. How many crates are on each lorry? ....

21. Which angle below is the best estimate for angle v: 40°, 115° or 200°?

.... °

22. What is the missing number?
1600 ÷ [?] = 40 ....

23. What is 82 333 – 21 000? ....

24. Round 112 873 to the nearest ten thousand. ....

25. What is the missing number in these equivalent fractions? Use the diagram to help you.
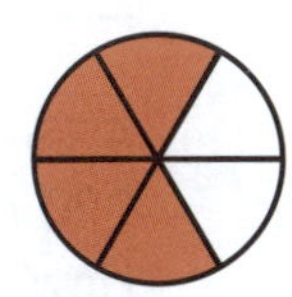
$\frac{4}{6} = \frac{2}{?}$ ....

26. Start at 576 243 and count up 3 steps of 100 000. What number do you get? ....

27. What is the missing number?
12 000 + [?] = 20 300 ....

28. Which number in the box is a common multiple of 6 and 8?

32 16 24 42

....

29. 29% of pupils in Year 5 wear glasses. What is this as a fraction? ....

30. Don paints for 2 hours each week for 3 weeks. How many minutes does he paint for in total? .... mins

Test 6

Part A

1. Which digit is in the ten thousands position of 10 763? ....

2. What is 31 291 ÷ 1000? ....

3. Start at –3 and count back 5. What number do you get? ....

4. 94 499 people live in Martsonville. How many people live there rounded to the nearest thousand? ....

5. What is the missing number?
   37 530 – [?] = 29 530 ....

6. What is the area of this shape?
   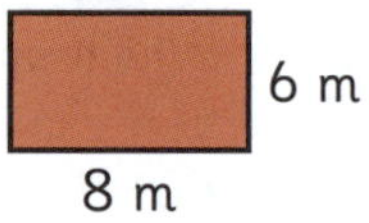

   .... m^2

7. 4 identical aeroplanes have a total of 412 seats. How many seats does each plane have? ....

8. What is 350 × 100? ....

9. Which of these is not a factor pair of 72?
   [8 and 9] [3 and 18] [6 and 12] ....

10. A farmer grows 1800 carrots. 220 are eaten by rabbits. How many carrots are left? ....

11. What is $\frac{2}{5} \times 2$?
    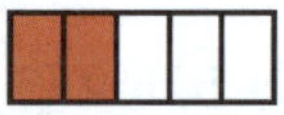
    Use the diagram to help you. ....

12. A school is split into 4 equal classes of 30 pupils. How many pupils are there in the school? ....

13. A diver scores 39.2 points. What is their score rounded to the nearest whole number? ....

14. What is the size of angle t?
    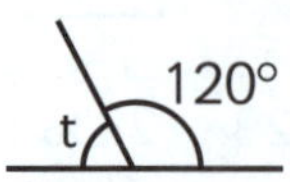

    .... °

15. Paddy has 350 trading cards. He shares them equally between 5 friends. How many cards does each friend get? ....

Part B

16. Use the diagram to help you find the missing number below.
    $\frac{10}{14} = \frac{5}{?}$
    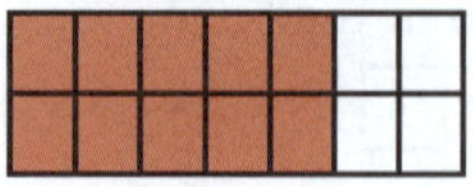
    ....

17. Chad saves £1.20 each day. How much does he save in a week? £....................

18. A rectangle has length 20 cm and height 14 cm. What is its perimeter? .... cm

19. Which symbol (< or >) should go in the box?
    0.92 [?] 0.94 ....

20. Start at 391 and count up 2 steps of 10. What number do you get? ....

21. This shape is made from 1 cm^3 cubes. How many more cubes are needed to give the shape a volume of 32 cm^3?

    ....

22. Find the missing number.
    $0.07 = \frac{?}{100}$ ....

23. What is 120 000 – 5200? ....

24. Write the first three multiples of 15. ....

25. What is the next term in this sequence?
    $\frac{4}{18}$, $\frac{7}{18}$, $\frac{10}{18}$, [?], ...

26. A polar bear is 1.6 m tall. How tall is this in cm?

    .... cm

27. What is the missing number?
    300 × [?] = 9000 ....

28. Write 0.47 as a fraction. ....

29. This timetable shows the departure times of some ferries. How many minutes are there between the departures of the Green and Blue ferries?

Green Ferry	10:50
Red Ferry	11:25
Blue Ferry	12:40

.... mins

30. Joel rode his bike every day for 49 days. How many weeks is this? .... weeks

Test 7

Warm Up Questions

The number cards show a 5-digit number. What number do you get if you swap the:

1) ones and thousands digits?

2) ten thousands and hundreds digits?

5	1	3	8	4

Part A

1. What is 9.8 rounded to the nearest whole number? ....

2. What is the missing number?
150 000 + [?] = 270 000 ....

3. What is the size of angle c? ....°

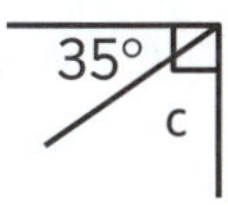

4. Which number in the box is a multiple of 8?

22	12	42	32

....

5. Use the diagram to help you work out $\frac{1}{3} \times 4$. Give your answer as an improper fraction. ....

6. An online shop sells 4 TVs every hour. How many TVs does it sell in a day? ....

7. What is the missing number?
840 ÷ [?] = 12 ....

8. Write 0.31 as a fraction. ....

9. It is 4 °C in Wallsend.
It is 12 °C colder in Dundee.
What is the temperature in Dundee? .... °C

10. What is 19 764 – 8400? ....

11. What is the perimeter of this shape? .... m

12. What is the missing number?

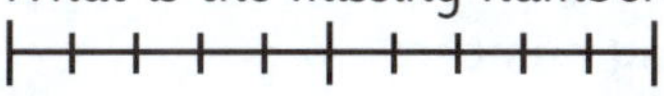

$\frac{15}{30}$ $\frac{?}{30}$ $\frac{25}{30}$ ....

13. Start at 9630 and count down 2 steps of 100. What number do you get? ....

Part B

14. The table shows how many pupils in each year group have brown hair. How many more pupils in Year 5 have brown hair than in Year 4?

Year 4	46
Year 5	61
Year 6	39

....

15. What is 562 × 1000? ....

16. Which symbol (< or >) should go in the box?
97.53 [?] 97.35 ....

17. Lisa has 5600 ml of water in her bucket.
She pours 600 ml more into it.
How much water is now in the bucket? .... ml

18. Use the diagram to work out the missing number in these equivalent fractions.
$\frac{6}{9} = \frac{?}{3}$ ....

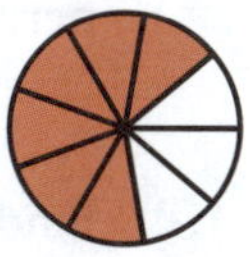

19. Carly plants 36 flowers in each flowerbed in her garden. How many flowers does she plant in 3 flowerbeds? ....

20. A bottle of water holds 1520 ml. How much is this in litres? l

21. What is 3% as a decimal? ....

22. A rectangle has length 9 cm and height 3 cm. What is its perimeter? .... cm

23. What is 6400 ÷ 8? ....

24. Which number is smaller?
56 571 or 56 617 ....

25. 14 children are given 12 sweets each. How many sweets are given in total? ....

Test 8

Part A

1. Which of these numbers is the smallest?
6.12   6.02   6.10   ....

2. A charity raises £143 295. What is this rounded to the nearest hundred thousand?   £..................

3. What are the common factors of 10 and 25?   .... and ....

4. What is the missing number in these equivalent fractions?

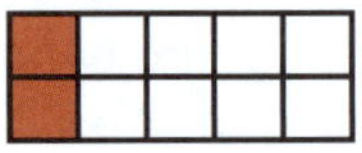

$\frac{2}{10} = \frac{?}{5}$ ....

5. A bag of sugar weighs 1000 g. How much do 13 bags weigh?   .... g

6. What is 64% as a decimal?   ....

7. Brian read 24 books in a year. Beth read a third of this number. How many books did Beth read?   ....

8. What is the area of this shape?

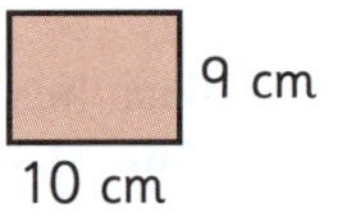

.... cm^2

9. A square photo frame has a perimeter of 48 cm. What is the length of one side of the frame?   .... cm

10. Find the missing number.
$0.06 = \frac{?}{100}$ ....

11. India buys 9 identical packs of crayons. There are 198 crayons altogether. How many are in each pack?   ....

12. A stack of paper is 320 mm thick. How thick is this in cm?   .... cm

13. An aeroplane flies 11 234 km one day, then 7040 km the next day. How far does it fly in total?   .... km

14. What is the size of angle e?

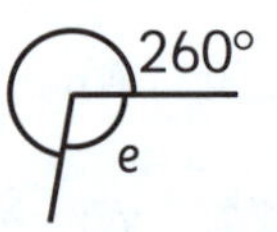

.... °

15. Nikki started a run at 7:00 am and finished at 7:40 am. Tom ran for three times as long as Nikki. How many hours did Tom run for?   .... hours

Part B

16. Look at this bus timetable. It takes 12 minutes to get from Hull Road to Rougier Street. What time does the bus leave from Hull Road?

Heslington	12:04
Hull Road	?
Rougier St.	12:23

....

17. What is the missing number?
284 320 – [?] = 54 320   ....

18. What is 14 000 + 2050?   ....

19. What number do you get when you count forwards 7 from –11?   ....

20. Write down the first three multiples of 22.   ....

21. What is 652 ÷ 10?   ....

22. What is $\frac{7}{100} \times 9$?
Use the diagram to help you.

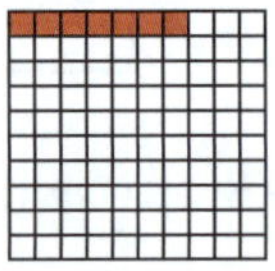

....

23. A poodle scores 5.6 points in a dog show. What is its score rounded to the nearest whole number?   ....

24. Start at 2317 and count up 8 steps of 1000. What number do you get?   ....

25. Which digit is in the thousands position of 45 328?   ....

26. There are 24 sweets in a bag. How many sweets are there in 5 bags?   ....

27. What is the next term in this sequence?
$\frac{8}{30}, \frac{13}{30}, \frac{18}{30},$ [?], ...

28. This shape is made from 1 cm^3 cubes. How many more cubes are needed to give the shape a volume of 45 cm^3?

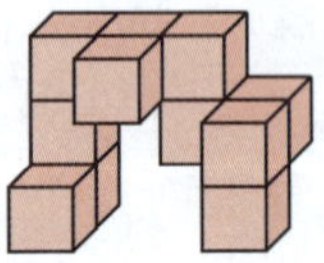

....

29. What is the missing number?
5 × [?] = 150   ....

30. Li shares 1680 ml of lemonade equally between 8 glasses. How much lemonade is in each glass?   .... ml

Test 9

Part A

1. Which symbol (< or >) should go in the box?
   19.19 [?] 19.91 ....

2. What are the common factors of 8 and 22? .... and ....

3. Find the missing number.
   $0.64 = \frac{?}{100}$ ....

4. What is 52 330 ÷ 1000? ....

5. Use the diagram to work out the missing number in these equivalent fractions.
   $\frac{3}{9} = \frac{?}{3}$ ....

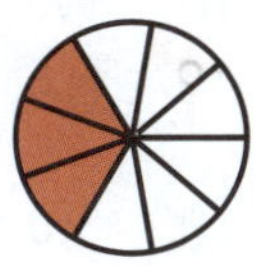

6. A punnet of raspberries weighs 255 g. How much do 10 punnets weigh? .... g

7. Amy saves 30p every day. She starts with £3.50. How much does she have after 10 days? £..................

8. What is the missing number?
   24 300 – [?] = 23 800 ....

9. It is –8 °C in Toronto. It is 12 °C warmer in Dublin. What is the temperature in Dublin? .... °C

10. Which angle below is the best estimate for angle w: 50°, 330° or 225°? .... °

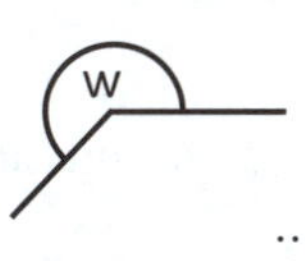

11. What is the missing number?
    1200 ÷ [?] = 60 ....

12. A rectangle has length 12 cm and height 2 cm. What is its area? .... cm^2

13. A canteen serves 690 potatoes at lunch. Each person served gets 3 potatoes. How many people are there? ....

14. What is the missing number?

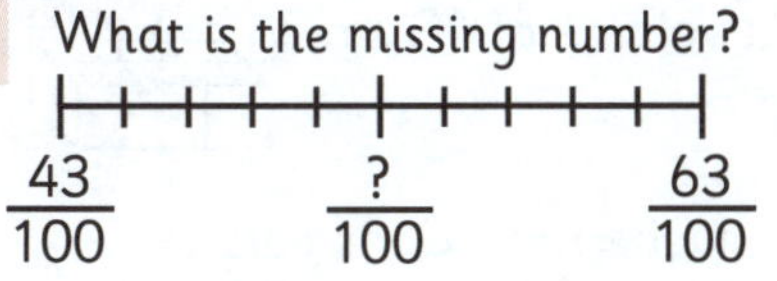

....

15. What is 5612 – 409? ....

Part B

16. A tennis club is open for 20 weeks of the year. How many days is this? .... days

17. What is the perimeter of this shape? .... cm

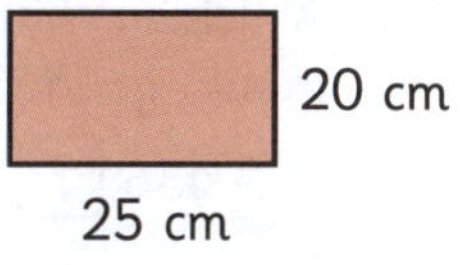

18. An emperor penguin weighs 35 kg. How much does it weigh in g? .... g

19. Which number in the box is a common multiple of 9 and 12?
    [60 36 81 96] ....

20. What is 18% as a decimal? ....

21. What is 6 × 120? ....

22. Neil has two bags of flour. There is 2481 g of flour in one bag and 3100 g in the other. How much flour does he have altogether? .... g

23. Round 648 366 to the nearest hundred thousand. ....

24. Work out $\frac{1}{8} \times 5$. Use the diagram to help you. ....

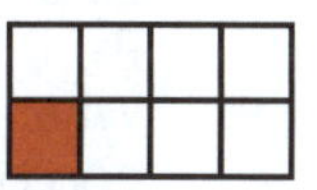

25. Start at 39 200 and count up 5 steps of 1000. What number do you get? ....

26. What is 4.3 rounded to the nearest whole number? ....

27. What is 305 ÷ 5? ....

28. Which digit is in the ten thousands position of 98 245? ....

29. A notebook is 118 mm thick. How thick is it in cm? .... cm

30. The table shows how many seconds it took 3 friends to run around a field. How much longer did Anita take than Anton?

Anton	72
Maria	85
Anita	98

.... s

Test 10

Part A

1. Round 67 523 to the nearest thousand. ....

2. Which symbol (< or >) should go in the box?
182 456 [?] 182 645 ....

3. Which of these is a factor pair of 63?
[4 and 8] [3 and 6] [7 and 9] ....

4. Start at 29 811 and count up 4 steps of 10 000. What number do you get? ....

5. Ella scores 59% on a test. What is her score out of 100 marks? ....

6. What is the area of this shape?

8 cm
11 cm

.... cm^2

7. An aeroplane flew 15 800 km. It stopped to refuel after 8000 km. How far did it have left to fly? .... km

8. A building has 90 floors. There are 20 windows on each floor. How many windows does the building have in total? ....

9. What is the missing number?
200 000 + [?] = 410 000 ....

10. What is 36.8 rounded to the nearest whole number? ....

11. 56 grapes are shared equally between 14 people. How many grapes does each person get? ....

12. What is the missing number in these equivalent fractions? Use the diagram to help you.
$\frac{4}{8} = \frac{2}{?}$

....

13. Sandeep jogs 5.23 km. How far is this in m? .... m

14. What is 762 ÷ 10? ....

15. Savina cooks some carrots for 5 minutes. She then adds beans and cooks for a further 2 and a half minutes. How many seconds does she cook for? .... s

Part B

16. A shop sold 50 sandwiches. Their fillings are shown in the table. How many egg sandwiches were sold?

Filling	Number of sandwiches
Egg	?
Tuna	17
Ham	23

....

17. Which of these numbers is the smallest?
12.23 13.12 12.32 ....

18. Work out $\frac{1}{9} \times 5$.
Use the diagram to help you. ....

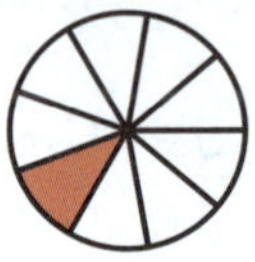

19. Start at 2 and count back 9. What number do you get? ....

20. A square has a perimeter of 80 cm. What is the length of one side? .... cm

21. Write the first three multiples of 30. ....

22. Andy has 6870 ml of water in his bucket. Juliet has 3100 ml in hers. How much water do they have altogether? .... ml

23. Write 0.97 as a fraction. ....

24. What is the size of angle k? .... °

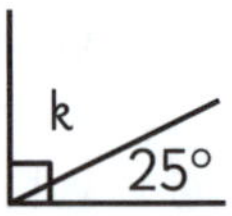

25. What is the missing number?
81 × [?] = 243 ....

26. What is 129 × 100? ....

27. One laptop costs £610. How much do three laptops cost? £..................

28. What is the next term in this sequence?
$\frac{23}{50}, \frac{30}{50}, \frac{37}{50},$ [?], ...

29. Each cube has a volume of 1 cm^3. How many more cubes are needed to give the shape a volume of 19 cm^3?

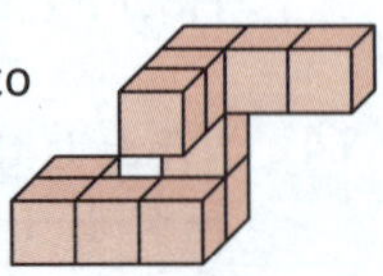

....

30. Donna eats 24 blueberries. Chris eats three quarters of this number. How many blueberries does Chris eat? ....

Test 11

Warm Up Questions

The box shows the factors of 30.

1) Which of these numbers are also factors of 33?

2) Which two of the numbers in the box have a common multiple of 8?

1	2	3	5
6	10	15	30

Part A

1. Write the first three multiples of 16. ....

2. What is 51 × 100? ....

3. Which digit is in the thousands position of 20 175? ....

4. It is 8 °C in Truro.
It is 10 °C colder in Wallsend.
What is the temperature in Wallsend? .... °C

5. Use the diagram to find the missing number in these equivalent fractions.

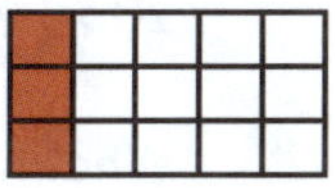

$\frac{3}{15} = \frac{?}{5}$ ....

6. Start at 7993 and count back 8 steps of 10. What number do you get? ....

7. What is 2.7 rounded to the nearest whole number? ....

8. Convert 9830 m to km. .... km

9. What is the size of angle g? .... °

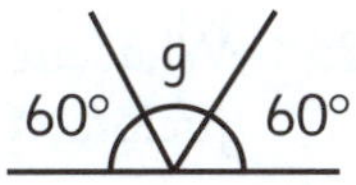

10. A library has 4820 books. The books are shared equally between 4 rooms. How many books are in each room? ....

11. What is the missing number?

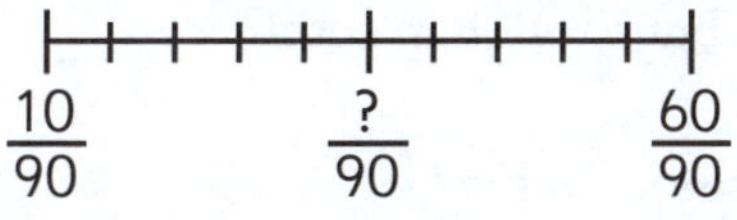

....

12. A set of headphones costs £45. How much do 8 sets cost? £..........

13. What is the missing number?
3600 ÷ [?] = 120 ....

Part B

14. Charlie's bucket can hold 9 litres of water. How much is this in ml? .... ml

15. What is 15 810 + 11 000? ....

16. What is the area of this shape? .... m^2

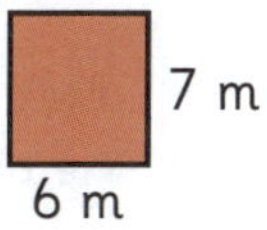

17. Find the missing number.
$0.7 = \frac{?}{10}$ ....

18. Amina is 9 and a half years old.
Kevin is 10 years and 1 month old.
How many months older is Kevin than Amina? .... months

19. What is 2950 – 1800? ....

20. Work out $\frac{1}{4} \times 3$.

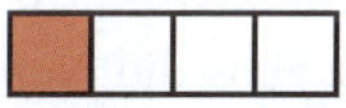

Use the diagram to help you. ....

21. Marius uses 168 beads to make 8 identical necklaces. How many beads are on each necklace? ....

22. Which of these numbers is the biggest?
41.11 41.41 41.14 ....

23. A rectangle has length 11 cm and height 6 cm. What is its perimeter? .... cm

24. What is the missing number?
106 000 – [?] = 66 000 ....

25. Use the train timetable to work out how long the shortest journey between Bristol and Plymouth is.

	Bristol	Plymouth
Train 1	09:25	10:17
Train 2	09:51	10:35

.... mins

Test 12

Part A

1. Which number is bigger:
871 395 or 871 539? ....

2. What is 15.2 rounded to the nearest whole number? ....

3. Work out $\frac{2}{11} \times 3$. 
Use the diagram to help you. ....

4. Which symbol (< or >) should go in the box?
21.79 [?] 21.81  ....

5. Alex has 1791 ml of squash in a bottle. He drinks 1500 ml. How much is left? .... ml

6. A flower is 120 mm tall. How tall is it in cm? .... cm

7. What is the perimeter of this shape? .... m

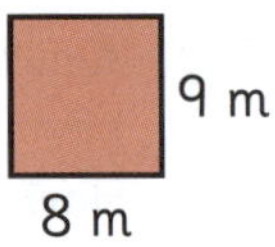

8. Write 0.13 as a fraction. ....

9. Leonie watched 35 films last year. Nardeep watched a fifth of this number. How many films did Nardeep watch? ....

10. A shop sells 3 identical TVs for a total of £9000. How much does one TV cost? £....................

11. What is 99 ÷ 100? ....

12. Lucie feeds 50 g of lettuce to each of her 3 guinea pigs. How much lettuce does she feed them in total? .... g

13. Which number in the box is a multiple of 8?

53	26	18	64

....

14. What is 86 × 1000? ....

15. Each cube has a volume of 1 cm^3. How many more cubes are needed to give the shape a volume of 22 cm^3?  ....

Part B

16. Look at Reena's school timetable. Art is 40 minutes long. If there are no breaks between lessons, what time does Music start?

Maths	13:30
Art	14:15
Music	?

....

17. What is the next term in this sequence?
$\frac{3}{16}, \frac{5}{16}, \frac{7}{16},$ [?], ...

18. What is 370 800 + 210 000? ....

19. A square has a side length of 5 m. What is its area? .... m^2

20. Round 102 873 to the nearest ten. ....

21. What is the missing number?
20 × [?] = 800 ....

22. What number do you get when you count forwards 6 from –4? ....

23. What is the missing number in these equivalent fractions? Use the diagram to help you.
$\frac{9}{12} = \frac{3}{?}$ .... 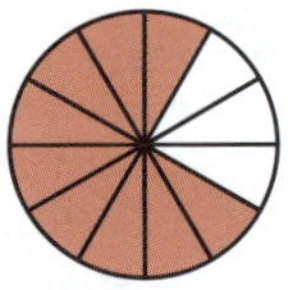

24. Start at 9323 and count back 2 steps of 1000. What number do you get? ....

25. What are the common factors of 9 and 12? .... and ....

26. What is the size of angle r? .... °

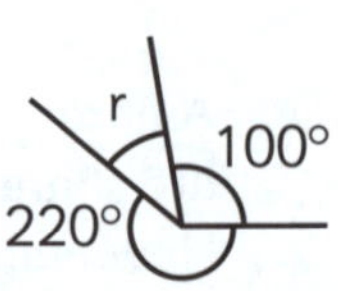

27. A bag of bird seed weighs 310 g. How much do 8 bags weigh in total? .... g

28. What is the missing number?
28 500 + [?] = 38 600 ....

29. What is 90% as a decimal? ....

30. A wheel of cheese is left to mature for 4 days. How many hours is this? .... hours

Section 1 Progress Test

1) The population of Kenforth is 256 912.

Which digit is in the ten thousands position? [ ] 1 mark

Round the population to the nearest hundred thousand. [ ] 1 mark

2) Which of the following weights is the heaviest?

72.60 kg   72.65 kg   72.51 kg

[ ] kg 1 mark

3) What number completes the equivalent fractions below?

$\frac{12}{16} = \frac{?}{4}$

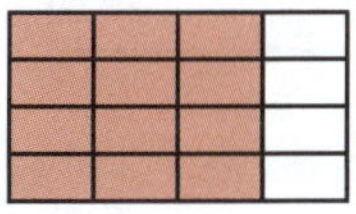

[ ]

$\frac{12}{20} = \frac{3}{?}$

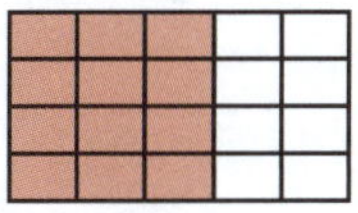

[ ] 2 marks

4) Look at the diagram on the right.

What is the size of angle a? [ ] ° 1 mark

What is the size of angle b? [ ] ° 1 mark

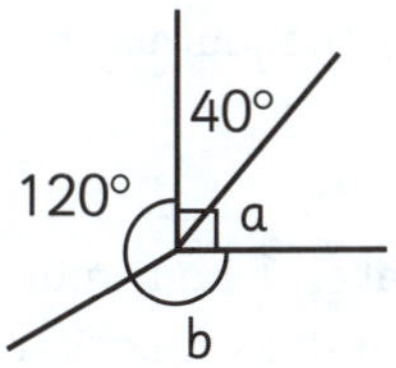

5) Complete the calculations below.

18 465 – 5040 = [ ] 1 mark

234 281 + 100 300 = [ ] 1 mark

Section 1 Progress Test

6) Annie scores 31 marks out of 50 on a test.

What is her score as a percentage?

%

1 mark

7) A field has a perimeter of 450 m.

How far is this in kilometres?

km

1 mark

Kamal runs 5 laps of the field. How far does he run in total?

m

1 mark

8) 2412 ml of juice is shared equally between 12 cups.

What volume of juice is in each cup?

ml

1 mark

9) Look at this timetable for trains travelling from York to Leeds.

How does the journey by Train 1 take?

mins

	York	Leeds
Train 1	13:55	14:32
Train 2	09:51	?

1 mark

Train 2 takes 1 hour and 16 minutes.
What time does it arrive?

1 mark

10) Look at the shape on the right.

What is the perimeter of this shape?

cm

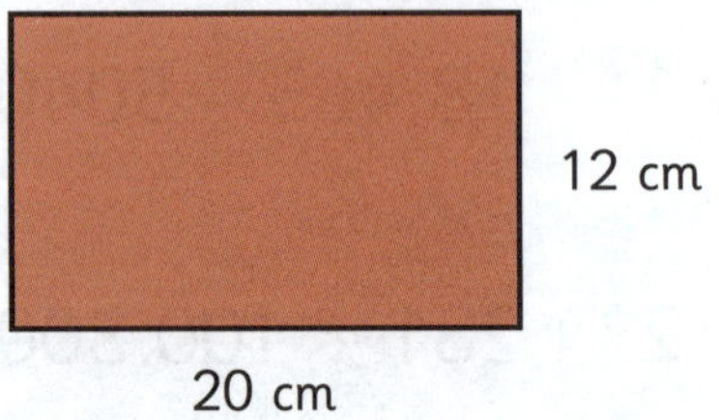

1 mark

What is the area of this shape?

cm^2

1 mark

Section 1 Listening Tests

Go to cgpbooks.co.uk/MA-Year5 or scan the QR code on the right to find the audio files for these listening tests. Listen carefully to each question before writing down your answer in the spaces provided for each test.

Each test has ten questions. You will have 5 seconds to answer each of the first five questions, and 10 seconds to answer each of the last five questions.

Section 1 Listening Tests

Listening Test 1

1. .... 2. .... 3. .... 4. ....

5. .... 6. .... 7. ....

8. £ .... 9. .... g 10. .... days

Barrow	07:43
Dalton	?
Kendal	08:59

Listening Test 2

1. .... 2. .... 3. .... 4. ....

5. .... 6. .... cm 7. ....

8. .... 9. .... cm 10. .... °

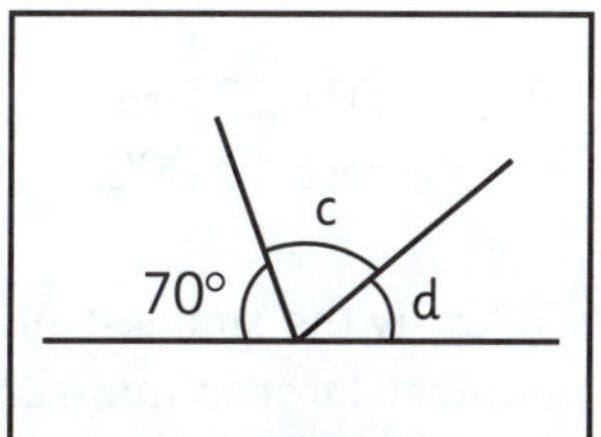

Listening Test 3

1. .... 2. .... 3. .... 4. ....

5. .... l 6. .... 7. ....

8. .... cm^2 9. .... 10. ....

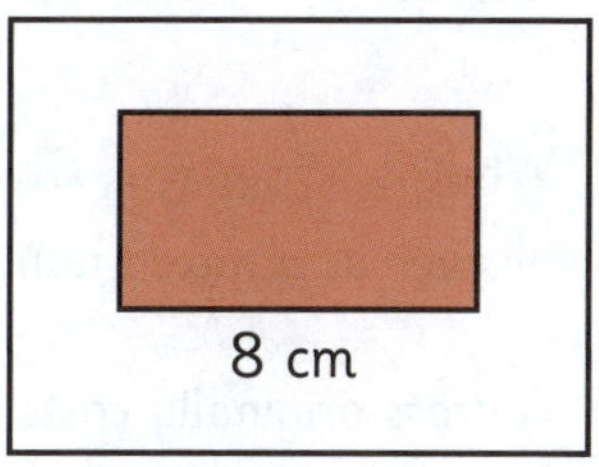

Test 1

Part A

1. What is 5.72 centimetres in millimetres? .... mm

2. Write down a multiple of 12 between 40 and 50. ....

3. What is $\frac{1}{5}$ more than $\frac{3}{5}$? ....

4. This line graph shows the temperature of a furnace one evening. How much did the temperature go down between 6 pm and 10 pm? .... °C

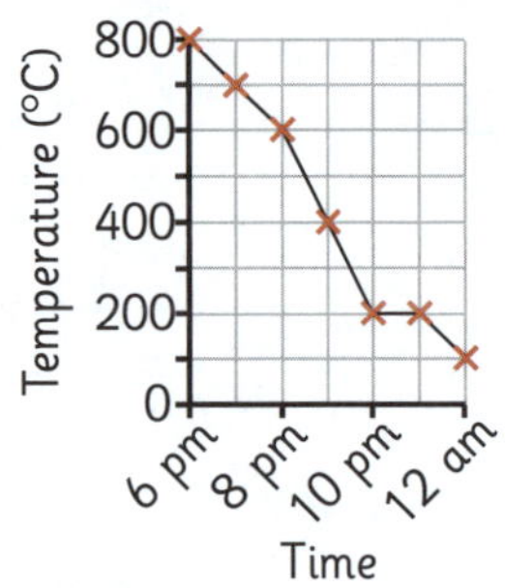

5. What is the Roman numeral CCV as a number? ....

6. What is 14 140 + 17 000? ....

7. A bird takes off from the ground. It flies 720 m up then 0.5 km down. How high up is the bird in kilometres? .... km

8. What is 7000 × 20? ....

9. Round 701 274 to the nearest 10 000. ....

10. What is the smallest prime number larger than 42? ....

11. What is $\frac{2}{5} \times 3$ as a mixed number? ....

12. Morris the cat weighs 4.47 kg. How much does he weigh to the nearest kilogram? .... kg

13. A rectangle has a width of 7 cm and a length of 11 cm. What is its area? .... cm^2

14. What is $4\frac{7}{9} - \frac{5}{9}$? Give your answer as a mixed number. ....

15. A dress originally costs £32.50. Jacqui buys it in a sale with £5 off. She uses a £20 gift card and pays the rest in cash. How much does Jacqui pay in cash? £..........

Part B

16. Write down a common factor of 45 and 27 that is bigger than 4. ....

17. The visitors at a zoo vote for their favourite animal. $\frac{1}{5}$ of visitors vote for the rhino. What is this as a percentage? .... %

18. Which fraction is smaller: $\frac{6}{7}$ or $\frac{11}{14}$? ....

19. How many steps of 100 000 are there between 913 801 and 113 801? ....

20. How many degrees are there in two whole turns? .... °

21. What is $\frac{8}{5}$ written as a mixed number? ....

22. 32 140 + [?] = 53 240
What is the missing number? ....

23. Which is longer: 70 cm or 30 inches? Use the approximation 5 centimetres ≈ 2 inches. ....

24. There is –£10 in a bank account. £12 is paid into the account. How much money is in the account now? £..........

25. This rectangle has a perimeter of 16 cm. What is the length of side a?

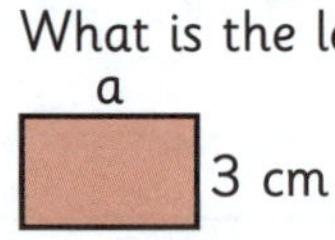

.... cm

26. Calculate 584 ÷ 8. ....

27. Work out the missing number to complete these equivalent fractions.
$\frac{16}{20} = \frac{8}{?}$ ....

28. Elva thinks of a number. She multiplies it by 9 and then subtracts 43 to get 137. What number is Elva thinking of? ....

29. Daisy does a tap class for 80 minutes and a jazz class for 1 hour and 10 minutes. How many minutes is this in total? .... mins

30. Work out the missing number in this calculation. 18.047 × [?] = 1804.7 ....

Test 2

Warm Up Questions

1) How many minutes is 180 seconds?
2) Dan starts brushing his teeth at the time shown on the clock. What time is this?
3) He brushes his teeth for 180 seconds. What time does he finish?

Part A

1. What is 70.26 × 100? ....

2. Which of the numbers in the box below is bigger than 2.20 but smaller than 3.15?

2.18	3.20	2.62	3.16

   ....

3. Write down a prime number between 33 and 40. ....

4. What is the size of angle E in this diagram? .... °

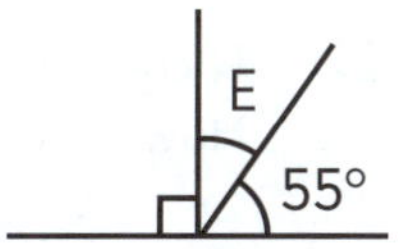

5. In a relay race, Kim runs 205 m, Molly-Mae runs 410 m and Karl runs 165 m. How far do they run in total? .... m

6. What is the next fraction in this sequence?
   $\frac{1}{8}, \frac{1}{4}, \frac{3}{8}, \boxed{?}, \ldots$ ....

7. Karim runs laps of the park for 1 hour and 15 minutes. Each lap takes him exactly 15 minutes. How many laps does he do in total? ....

8. 910 = $\boxed{?}$MX
   What is the missing Roman numeral? ....

9. Which of these fractions is the biggest:
   $\frac{3}{8}$, $\frac{5}{8}$ or $\frac{17}{24}$? ....

10. 100 g ≈ 4 oz. Approximately how many ounces is 800 grams? .... oz

11. Count forwards 3 from –7.
    What number do you get? ....

12. What is $\frac{32}{20} - \frac{9}{20}$? Give your answer as an improper fraction. ....

Part B

13. What is 3.29 rounded to the nearest whole number? ....

14. What is $3\frac{3}{7}$ written as an improper fraction? ....

15. A basketball weighs 600 g. What is the mass of 4 basketballs in kilograms? .... kg

16. Work out the perimeter of this shape. .... m

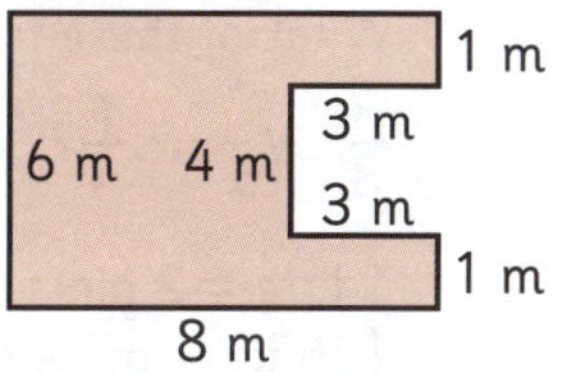

17. Work out 1320 ÷ 120. ....

18. Which amount is larger:
    4.1 kg or 4010 g? ....

19. 39% of Lola's jumpers are knitted.
    What is this as a fraction? ....

20. A rectangle has an area of 40 m^2 and a width of 5 m. What is its length? .... m

21. Three classes voted for their favourite pet. The results are shown in the table. Which pet got the fewest votes in Class 5Y?

Class	5X	5Y	5Z
Cat	12	6	10
Dog	7	15	4

    ....

22. 344 219 – $\boxed{?}$ = 44 219
    What is the missing number? ....

23. Which factor of 81 isn't in the box below?

1	3	27	81

    ....

24. Work out 298 940 – 70 003. ....

Test 3

Part A

1. What is 515 ÷ 5? ....

2. What is the biggest multiple of 3 between 60 and 70? ....

3. What is 45% as a decimal? ....

4. A shape made from two rectangles has six sides of length 4 cm and 2 sides of length 5 cm. What is the perimeter of the shape? .... cm

5. Write 2007 as a Roman numeral. ....

6. Find a number in the box which is a common factor of 54 and 18.

4	6	8	12	14

....

7. What of these fractions is the smallest: $\frac{3}{8}$, $\frac{5}{16}$ or $\frac{1}{4}$? ....

8. 1 litre ≈ 2 pints. A bath can hold 126 litres of water. Approximately how much is this in pints? .... pints

9. 52 820 + [?] = 56 820
What is the missing number? ....

10. Count backwards 12 from 4. What number do you get? ....

11. Work out 44 935 + 8000. ....

12. The line graph shows how far Faryad fell in the first 20 seconds of a skydive. How far did Faryad fall in the first 10 seconds? .... m

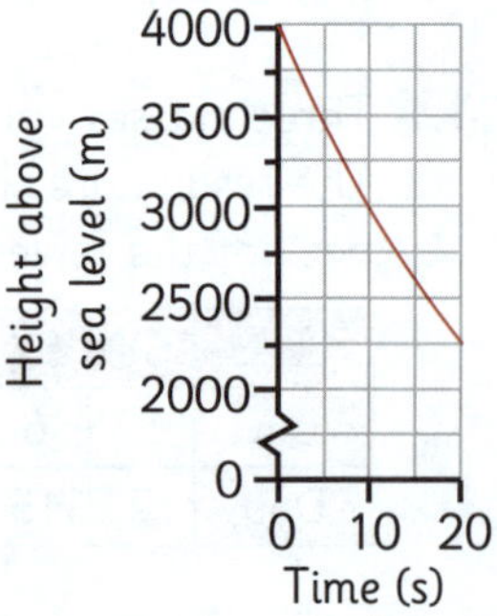

13. Which distance is largest: 7.5 km, 75 000 m or 7500 cm? ....

14. Jo throws away $\frac{1}{10}$ of her toys and gives another 40% to charity. What percentage of her toys does she have left? .... %

15. Calculate 92 × 3. ....

Part B

16. Work out 1854 – 600 + 340. ....

17. Which of these numbers is the smallest: 8.61, 8.59 or 8.64? ....

18. Work out the missing number to complete these equivalent fractions.
$\frac{9}{10} = \frac{?}{30}$ ....

19. Count up 2 steps of 100 from 318 421. What number do you get? ....

20. True or false? There are 5 prime numbers between 0 and 10. ....

21. What is $\frac{1}{3} \times 7$? Give your answer as a mixed number. ....

22. Nico is going to France in 98 days. How long is this in weeks? .... weeks

23. The number 653 924 is rounded to get 650 000. Has it been rounded to the nearest 10, 100, 1000 or 10 000? ....

24. What is the size of angle G in this diagram?

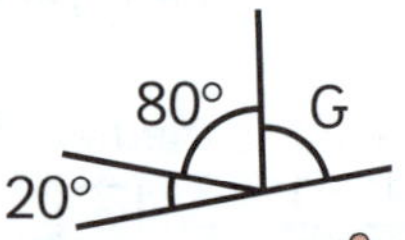

.... °

25. Minnie the monkey eats 1224 bananas in a year. She eats the same number of bananas each month. How many bananas does she eat each month? ....

26. Karol shares 2.4 litres of water equally between 3 bowls. How much water is in each bowl in millilitres? .... ml

27. What is 6.83 rounded to the nearest whole number? ....

28. What is $\frac{15}{10} + \frac{16}{10}$? Give your answer as a mixed number. ....

29. A rectangle has an area of 35 cm^2 and a length of 7 cm. What is its width? .... cm

30. In an election Ben got 62 votes and El got 5 times as many votes as Ben. How many more votes did El get than Ben? ....

Test 4

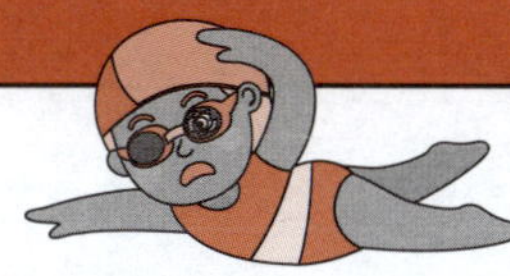

Part A

1. Work out 180.9 ÷ 1000. ....

2. Convert 5.82 litres to millilitres. .... ml

3. What is 246 440 – 20 000? ....

4. What is the missing number in this calculation? 86 ÷ [?] = 0.086 ....

5. Look at the shape on the right. What is the length of side a?

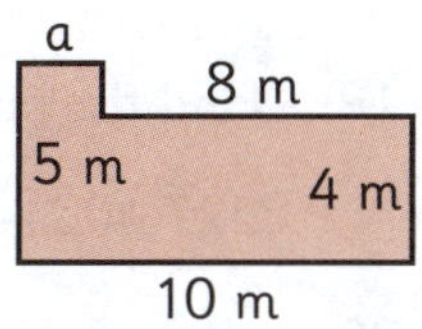

.... m

6. Work out $\frac{3}{10} \times 6$. Give your answer as an improper fraction. ....

7. 336 316 – [?] = 236 216
What is the missing number? ....

8. Tyler is selling boxes of strawberries. He has 819 strawberries. If Tyler puts 9 strawberries in each box, how many boxes will he need? ....

9. Look at this timetable for a cable car. On Sunday, the cable car arrives at the ski slopes 3 minutes before 11 am. What is the missing time in the timetable?

	Saturday	Sunday
Ice café	09:27	10:41
Ski slopes	09:43	?

....

10. What is 27 feet in metres? Use the approximation 1 metre ≈ 3 feet. .... m

11. Which factor of 16 isn't in the box below?

1 2 8 16

....

12. Jack has £9.52. How much money does he have to the nearest pound? £....................

13. Write 19 quarters as a mixed number. ....

14. In a game, players start with 2000 points. Tinaye loses 170 points in the first round and 1020 points in the second round. How many points does he have left? ....

15. Araf drinks $\frac{1}{4}$ of a 1 litre bottle of juice. How much is this as a decimal? l

Part B

16. Ella swims 10 lengths of a pool in 8 minutes and 20 seconds. Hiran takes 3 times as long as Ella. How many minutes does it take Hiran to swim 10 lengths? .... mins

17. It costs £81.30 to hire a bouncy castle for 3 days. How much would it cost for 6 days? £....................

18. Count down 6 steps of 1000 from 671 512. What number do you get? ....

19. 3000 × [?] = 360 000
What is the missing number? ....

20. Which of these fractions is not equivalent to the others: $\frac{3}{4}$, $\frac{30}{40}$ or $\frac{60}{100}$? ....

21. A kitchen makes 40 pizzas. Each pizza is decorated with 7 tomatoes. How many tomatoes are used in total? ....

22. Dana is on floor 8 of a shopping centre. She goes down 10 floors to the car park. What floor is she on now? ....

23. Round 529 441 to the nearest 100 000. ....

24. What is the area of the square with side length 9 m? .... m^2

25. What is the next fraction in this sequence?
$\frac{7}{10}$, $\frac{1}{2}$, $\frac{3}{10}$, [?], ...

26. Which letter in the grid shows the new position of Shape A after it is translated 3 squares left and 3 squares up?

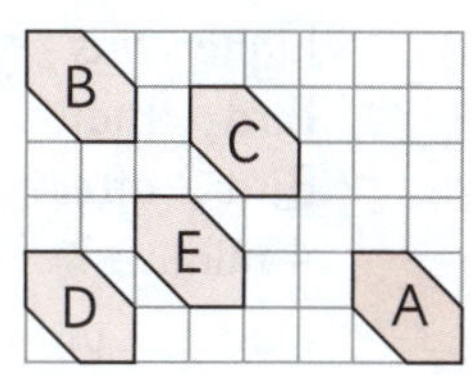

....

27. Which of these numbers is the biggest: 11.07, 10.89 or 11.13? ....

28. Ed's book has 100 pages. Ed prints 3 copies each of his book for 6 of his friends. How many pages does he print? ....

29. Work out the missing number to complete the fraction: 94% = $\frac{?}{100}$ ....

30. Write down a prime number between 50 and 55. ....

Test 5

Part A

1. What number is 4 steps of 100 up from 48 539? ....

2. Work out 4210 + 2000. ....

3. Count backwards to work out 2 – 7. ....

4. Find angle G.

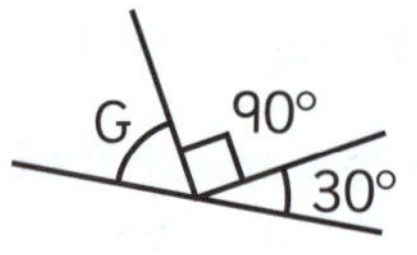

.... °

5. Which fraction is smaller, $\frac{3}{10}$ or $\frac{1}{5}$? ....

6. 1 litre ≈ 2 pints. Approximately how many pints is 44 litres? .... pints

7. Find the missing number:

   8.23 × [?] = 82.3 ....

8. Munir sells three CDs for £4.60 each. How much does he earn in total from selling the CDs? £..................

9. Write out the first five multiples of 7.

   ...., ..., ..., ..., ...

10. Write 17% as a fraction with denominator 100. ....

11. What is the missing number?

    1100 × [?] = 66 000 ....

12. How much higher was Bird 1 than Bird 2 after 4 minutes?

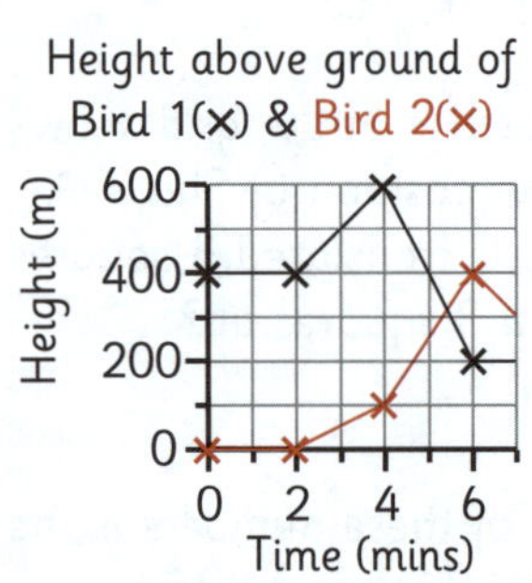

.... m

13. Harry has 180 flowers. He divides them into 12 equal bunches. How many flowers are in each bunch? ....

14. Find $\frac{22}{7} - \frac{9}{7}$. Give your answer as an improper fraction. ....

15. A rectangle has an area of 60 m². Its length is 5 m. What is its width? .... m

Part B

16. It takes Mila 15 minutes to eat breakfast. How many hours does she spend eating breakfast over 8 days? .... hours

17. Convert 12 000 g to kilograms. .... kg

18. What is $\frac{7}{10}$ × 8? Give your answer as an improper fraction. ....

19. Find the missing number:

    227 402 – [?] = 57 402 ....

20. Uma cycled 10 029 m on Saturday and 15 143 m on Sunday. How much further did she cycle on Sunday than Saturday? .... m

21. What is 52 ÷ 100? ....

22. Write $2\frac{2}{3}$ as an improper fraction. ....

23. Round 945 621 to the nearest 100 000. ....

24. What is the perimeter of this shape?

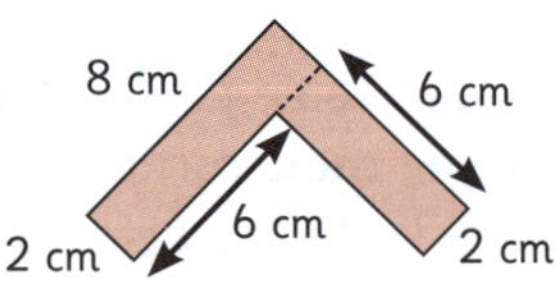

.... cm

25. Find the missing number:

    500 × [?] = 250 000 ....

26. Caleb buys 32 packs of crayons. Each pack has 5 different colours and contains 2 of each colour. How many crayons are there in total? ....

27. Which fraction is not equivalent to the others?

    $\frac{10}{100}$ $\frac{2}{5}$ $\frac{5}{50}$

    ....

28. Put these decimals in order, starting with the largest:

    4.872   4.8   4.806

    ...., ..., ...

29. What prime number is between 85 and 90? ....

30. What is the year 1308 as a Roman numeral? ....

Test 6

Warm Up Questions

The table shows the depth compared to sea level of some creatures:

Whale	–27 m
Dolphin	–14 m
Shark	–19 m

1) Which creature is closest to 0 m?

2) Which creature is swimming the deepest?

Part A

1. Write $\frac{3}{100}$ as a decimal. ....

2. Find the missing number:
   1400 ÷ [?] = 140 ....

3. Work out 4921 – 2400. ....

4. What is the largest number with two decimal places that is less than 29.8? ....

5. Write 9 fifths as a mixed number. ....

6. Find the missing number:
   68 160 + [?] = 98 960 ....

7. How long does it take the cyclist to travel from 20 km to 50 km from home?

   .... hour(s)

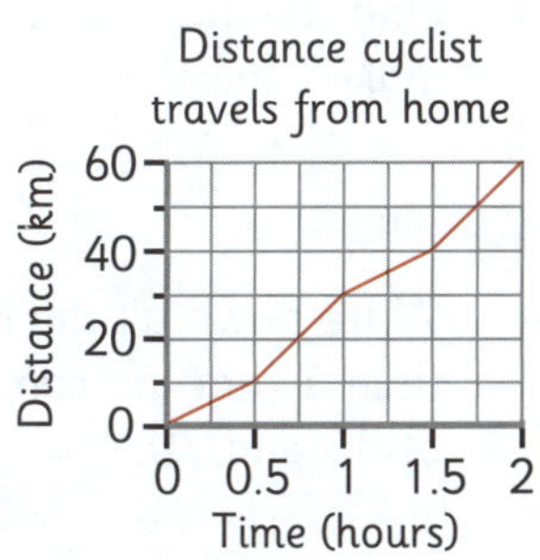

8. What is the missing Roman numeral?
   850 = DCC[?]L ....

9. Fran's daisy chain is 30 cm long.
   Lucy's daisy chain is $\frac{5}{6}$ times as long.
   How long is Lucy's daisy chain? .... cm

10. What is the smallest prime number that's bigger than 12? ....

11. 1 metre ≈ 3 feet. Approximately how many metres is 33 feet? .... m

12. Which decimal below rounds to a different whole number from the others?

12.57	12.97	13.56

    ....

13. What is 40.83 × 10? ....

Part B

14. What is the missing number?
    $\frac{8}{9} + \frac{7}{9} = 1\frac{?}{9}$ ....

15. Harrison buys 7 packs of bubblegum. Each pack has 12 pieces. How many pieces are left in total after he has chewed 6 pieces? ....

16. Write down the two numbers that are 3 steps of 10 from 290 567.

    .... and ....

17. What is the size of angle B?

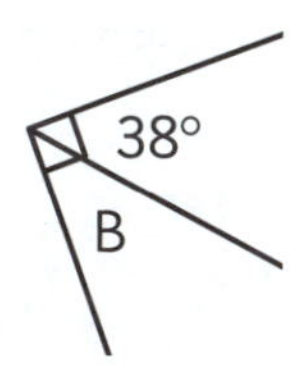

    ....°

18. An apple tree is 320 cm tall. A pear tree is three times as tall as the apple tree. How tall is the pear tree? .... cm

19. Safia is 64 months old. How old is she in years and months?

    .... years and .... months

20. The numbers below are the factors of 18. What number is missing?

1	2	?	6	9	18

    ....

21. Round 638 746 to the nearest 100. ....

22. Find the missing number to make equivalent fractions. $\frac{44}{100} = \frac{22}{?}$ ....

23. Convert 53 800 ml to litres. l

24. A square has an area of 36 cm^2. What is the length of one of its sides? .... cm

Test 7

Part A

1. What is 120 × 100? ....

2. What is the Roman numeral DXV as a number? ....

3. Convert 3100 m to kilometres. .... km

4. Find 25 820 – 7040. ....

5. Find the improper fraction that comes next in this sequence:
$\frac{1}{5}$, $\frac{3}{5}$, 1, [?] ....

6. What is 372 ÷ 4? ....

7. Mike is standing $3\frac{4}{7}$ m from a camera.
Gita is standing $\frac{3}{7}$ m closer than Mike.
How far is Gita from the camera?
Give your answer as a mixed number. .... m

8. Count forwards to work out –4 + 2. ....

9. Work out 231 941 + 50 009. ....

10. What is the perimeter of this shape?

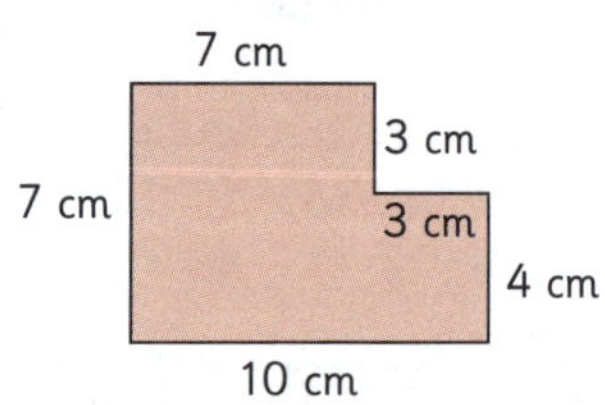

.... cm

11. Libbie thought of a number.
She multiplied it by 8,
and then subtracted 5.
The number she arrived at was 91.
What was her original number? ....

12. Find the missing number:
20 × [?] = 24 000 ....

13. Find $2\frac{1}{5}$ × 4. Give your answer as a mixed number. ....

14. Count in steps of 100 000 to find the missing numbers in this sequence:
141 532 .... 441 532

15. This is a train timetable. The 14:02 train from Ledford is 15 minutes late. When will it arrive in Malby?

Ledford	13:31	14:02
Colston	14:18	14:49
Malby	14:37	15:08

....

Part B

16. Find the missing number:
8400.5 ÷ [?] = 84.005 ....

17. A table is 750 mm long.
It is extended by 24 cm.
How long is the table now, in cm? .... cm

18. How many eighths are in $1\frac{7}{8}$? ....

19. 1 kilogram ≈ 2 pounds. Approximately how many kilograms is 90 pounds? .... kg

20. Find angle X.

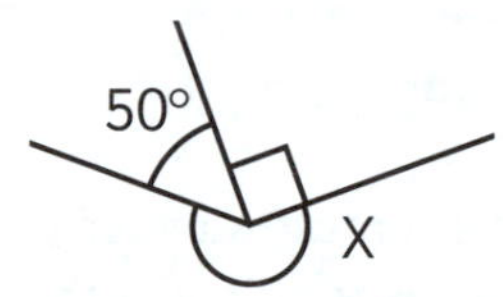

.... °

21. What is the only even prime number? ....

22. Jo cycles 29.85 km. How far does she cycle to the nearest km? .... km

23. Find the missing number to make equivalent fractions.
$\frac{5}{6} = \frac{?}{12}$ ....

24. Write down all the numbers greater than 1 that are common factors of 35 and 70.
....

25. Comics in a shop cost 99p each.
Jared wants to buy 6 comics.
How much will it cost him? £ ....

26. Which symbol (< or >) should go in the box?
7.395 [?] 7.299 ....

27. Write $\frac{4}{10}$ as a percentage. .... %

28. A rectangle has an area of 27 m^2.
Its height is 9 m. What is its length? .... m

29. Work out 37 700 – 23 650. ....

30. It took George 45 days to read a book.
How long is this in weeks and days?
.... weeks and .... days

Test 8

Part A

1. Round 427 509 to the nearest 1000. ....

2. What prime number is between 14 and 18? ....

3. What is 400 × 30? ....

4. Which of the numbers in the box are multiples of 8?

36	56	72	84	96

....

5. Ishaq has 1.4 kg of pasta. He evenly divides it between 7 dishes. How many grams of pasta is in each dish? .... g

6. Work out 29 534 – 10 300. ....

7. Find angle P.

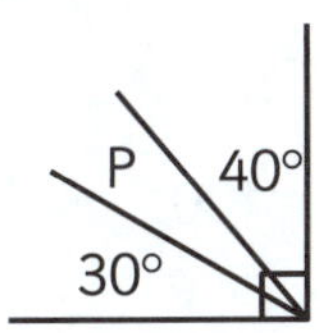

.... °

8. Erin finds 60 spiders in her garden. Each spider has 8 legs. How many legs do the spiders have altogether? ....

9. What number is one hundred times smaller than 52.1? ....

10. Write $\frac{11}{4}$ as a mixed number. ....

11. What is 90 ÷ 18? ....

12. A blue train travelled 46 000 miles last year. A red train travelled 30 900 miles more. How many miles did the red train travel? .... miles

13. A square has a perimeter of 32 m. What is the length of one of its sides? .... m

14. Which of the fractions below is largest?

$\frac{1}{2}$	$\frac{3}{8}$	$\frac{3}{4}$

....

15. Madeleine swam for an hour. How many seconds was she swimming for? .... s

16. Work out 112 320 + 209 000. ....

Part B

17. What is the smallest number with three decimal places that is more than 13.12? ....

18. 100 grams ≈ 4 ounces. Approximately how many grams is 40 ounces? .... g

19. Count forwards to work out –8 + 11. ....

20. A chef can chop $3\frac{1}{6}$ carrots in a minute. How many can he chop in 5 minutes? ....

21. Find the area of this shape.

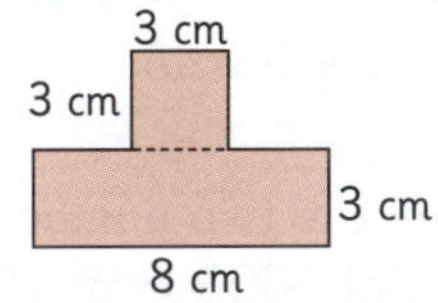

.... cm^2

22. Which Roman numeral is smaller, CCXX or CCXV? ....

23. A paint shop has 520 tins of paint. The shop sells one fifth of their paint in one day. How many tins of paint do they sell? ....

24. Convert 1165 cm to metres. .... m

25. Work out $3\frac{3}{5} + \frac{4}{5}$. Give your answer as a mixed number. ....

26. Find the missing number:

45.092 × [?] = 45 092 ....

27. Count in steps of 10 000 to find the missing numbers in this sequence:

388 578 .... 418 578

28. What is 109 537 – 450? ....

29. What is $\frac{1}{4}$ as a percentage? .... %

30. The number of apples in a shop is the same as the total number of melons and mangos. Use the table to find the number of mangos. ....

Fruit	Number
Melon	38
Apple	145
Mango	

Test 9

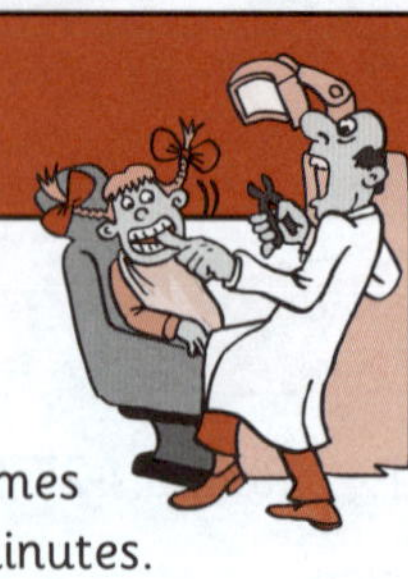

Part A

1. What is 17 370 – 4100? ....

2. What is the smallest prime number that is greater than 4? ....

3. Find the missing number:
$92 \times \boxed{?} = 9200$ ....

4. A horse eats 12 kg of hay a day. It eats a quarter of the hay in the morning. How many grams of hay does the horse eat in the morning? .... g

5. What is $\frac{3}{4} \times 5$? Give your answer as an improper fraction. ....

6. Write down the two numbers that are 4 steps of 1000 from 155 998.
.... and ....

7. Work out 54 ÷ 18. ....

8. What is the missing Roman numeral?
425 = C [?] XXV ....

9. What is the largest number with two decimal places that is less than 13.4? ....

10. Sachin uses 5 scoops of ice cream to make one milkshake. How many scoops would he use to make 80 milkshakes? ....

11. What is the size of angle D?

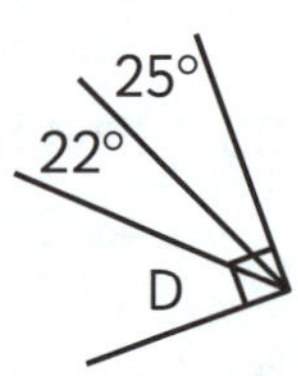

.... °

12. The numbers below are the factors of 20. What numbers are missing?

1	2	?	?	10	20

.... and ....

13. Round 73 862 to the nearest 100 000. ....

14. 1 kilogram ≈ 2 pounds. Approximately how many pounds is 35 kg? .... pounds

15. What number comes next in this sequence?
$3, \ 2\frac{1}{3}, \ 1\frac{2}{3}, \ \boxed{?}$ ....

Part B

16. Lucy went to see the dentist 3 times one year. Each visit lasted 10 minutes. How many seconds did Lucy spend at the dentist that year? .... s

17. How many quarters are there in $3\frac{3}{4}$? ....

18. What is the length of this rectangle?

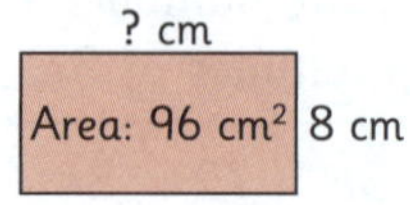

.... cm

19. Fraser has 825 ml of water. He gives 75 ml to his mouse. He shares the rest of the water equally between 3 rabbits. How many ml does each rabbit get? .... ml

20. Find the missing number to make equivalent fractions. $\frac{70}{100} = \frac{7}{?}$ ....

21. Work out 130.4 ÷ 100. ....

22. What is 8.96 km in metres? .... m

23. Count forwards to work out –5 + 13. ....

24. Anna and Yusuf are putting clothes in the same suitcase. Anna fills $\frac{2}{7}$ of the suitcase and Yusuf fills $\frac{4}{7}$. What fraction of the suitcase is empty? ....

25. Work out 43 × 7. ....

26. This is a bus timetable. If the journey times between places are always the same, what is the missing time?

Gately	Hilford	Ebdon
08:32	08:57	09:23
09:07	?	09:58

....

27. Find the missing number:
$43\,745 + \boxed{?} = 52\,752$ ....

28. What is the largest multiple of 11 that is less than 80? ....

29. What is the perimeter of a field with length 103 m and width 37 m? .... m

30. Write 61% as a fraction with denominator 100. ....

Test 10

Warm Up Questions

Look at this box of numbers.

601 520	620.3	6420
6203	64.2	6015.2

Which number is:

1) 10 times smaller than 642?

2) 100 times bigger than 62.03?

3) 1000 times bigger than 601.52?

Part A

1. What is $\frac{9}{10} + \frac{4}{10}$? Give your answer as an improper fraction. ....

2. Round 9.74 to the nearest whole number. ....

3. Write down all the numbers greater than 1 that are common factors of 42 and 56. ....

4. What is the perimeter of this shape? .... cm

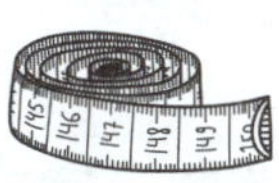

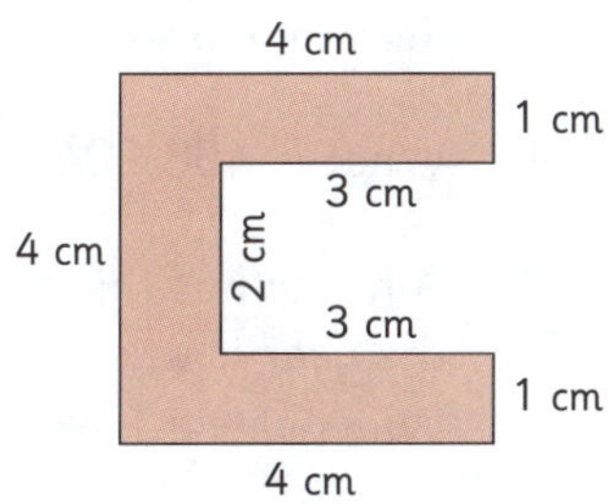

5. Find the missing number: 361 513 + [?] = 372 413 ....

6. Two angles make a half turn when they're put together. One angle is 110°. What is the other angle? ....°

7. 555 423 is rounded to get 555 400. Was it rounded to the nearest 10, 100 or 1000? ....

8. Which fraction is smaller, $\frac{1}{4}$ or $\frac{6}{20}$? ....

9. Count in steps of 10 000 to find the missing numbers in this sequence:

   242 153 .... 272 153

10. What is the Roman numeral CLX as a number? ....

11. Ling can do $1\frac{1}{2}$ turns when diving off the highest diving board. How many turns will she have done after 2 dives? ....

Part B

12. School shirts are sold in packs of 5. A factory has made 255 shirts. How many packs of 5 can they make? ....

13. Find 300 × 900. ....

14. Count backwards to work out −3 − 9. ....

15. What is the missing number? $20\% = \frac{?}{5}$ ....

16. It took a rocket 3 days to reach the moon. How many hours is this? .... hours

17. Write $2\frac{5}{8}$ as an improper fraction. ....

18. Work out 133 860 − 7600. ....

19. Which symbol (< or >) should go in the box? 6.112 [?] 6.15 ....

20. In what year was the trunk of Tree 1 2 cm wider than Tree 2? ....

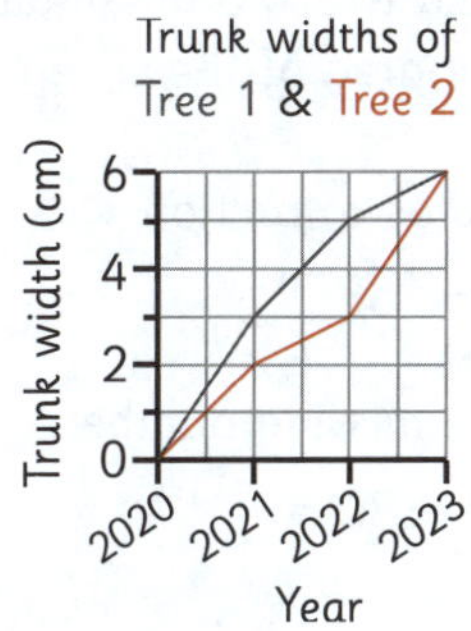

21. A bath contains 182 000 ml of water. How much is this in litres? l

22. A blue car costs £17 450. A silver car costs £13 020 more than the blue car. How much does the silver car cost? £..................

23. 100 grams ≈ 4 ounces. Approximately how many ounces is 600 grams? .... ounces

24. What is 270 ÷ 9? ....

Test 11

Part A

1. What is 32 500 + 1700? ....

2. Count backwards to work out –4 – 6. ....

3. Which number between 50 and 60 is a multiple of 9? ....

4. Find the missing number to make equivalent fractions. $\frac{3}{8} = \frac{?}{16}$ ....

5. What number is 3 steps of 10 000 up from 662 451? ....

6. A triangle has a corner at coordinates (6, 3). The triangle is translated 2 squares right and 1 square down. What are the coordinates of the corner now? ....

7. Work out 61 × 4. ....

8. What is $\frac{17}{6} - \frac{6}{6}$? Give your answer as a mixed number. ....

9. What is the perimeter of this shape?

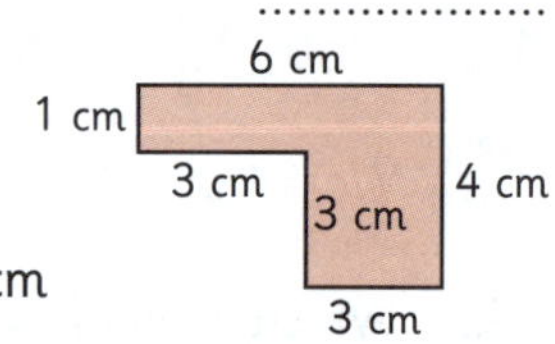

.... cm

10. A cow field has an area of 17 934 m^2. A sheep field is 5070 m^2 smaller. What is the area of the sheep field? .... m^2

11. Write 80% as a fraction in its simplest form. ....

12. What is the missing number? 640 ÷ [?] = 80 ....

13. What is the sum of the two smallest prime numbers? ....

14. After how many months does the monkey have a mass of 4 kg more than it did when it was born?

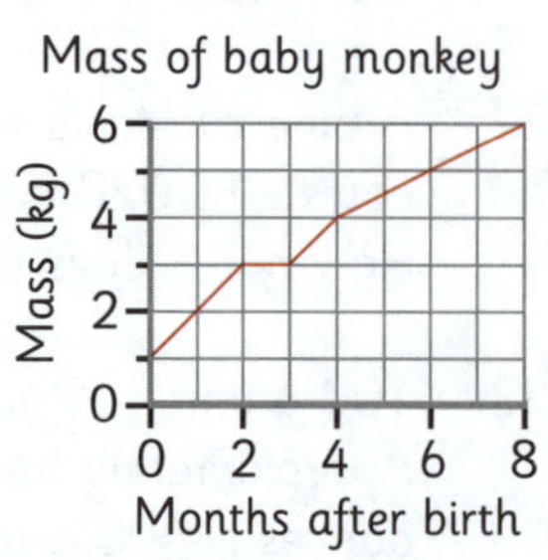

.... months

15. A pen is 13.25 cm long. How long is this in mm? .... mm

Part B

16. What is 4710.3 ÷ 10? ....

17. What is the size of angle W?

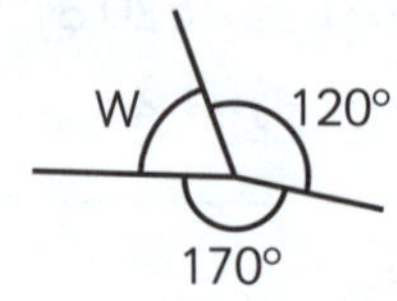

.... °

18. Joshua stood on one leg for 32 seconds. Mina stood on one leg for twice as long as Joshua. How long did Mina stand on one leg for, in minutes and seconds?

.... minute(s) and .... seconds

19. Find the missing number: 154 903 – [?] = 123 103 ....

20. What is the smallest number with three decimal places that is bigger than 8.8? ....

21. What is 458 904 + 30 200? ....

22. A house has this sign showing the year it was built: **MMIX**
When was it built? ....

23. 1 litre ≈ 2 pints. Approximately how many pints is 102 litres? .... pints

24. What is 60 000 ÷ 120? ....

25. Fiona got 50 cards at Christmas. She got $\frac{4}{5}$ as many cards on her birthday. How many cards did she get in total? ....

26. Round 629 712 to the nearest 1000. ....

27. Put these fractions in order, starting with the smallest.

$\frac{5}{12}$ $\frac{1}{3}$ $\frac{5}{6}$

....

28. What is the area of a piece of paper with width 12 cm and length 20 cm? .... cm^2

29. Find the missing number: 370 × [?] = 3700 ....

30. A witch puts 4.8 litres of potion in bottles. A bottle holds 1200 ml of potion. How many bottles are needed? ....

Test 12

Part A

1. Write $\frac{302}{1000}$ as a decimal. ....

2. Round 865 935 to the nearest 10 000. ....

3. Write $\frac{13}{8}$ as a mixed number. ....

4. 5 cm ≈ 2 inches. Approximately how many cm is 8 inches? .... cm

5. What is the area of this shape?

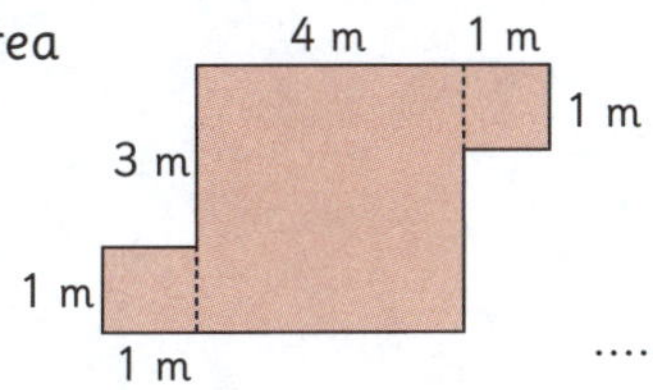

.... m^2

6. Aseem has 315 g of sweets. He shares them out equally between 3 people. How many grams do they get each? .... g

7. Which fraction is not equivalent to the others?

$\frac{5}{9}$	$\frac{12}{18}$	$\frac{2}{3}$

....

8. Find the missing number:
324 355 – [?] = 314 350 ....

9. What is 23 400 m in kilometres? .... km

10. Riley has 147 pictures of her cat. She uses them to make a 12-month calendar with 11 pictures for each month. If no pictures are repeated, how many aren't used? ....

11. Write $\frac{9}{50}$ as a percentage. .... %

12. Find the missing number:
980 ÷ [?] = 9.8 ....

13. Write 290 as a Roman numeral. ....

14. Put these decimals in order, starting with the largest:
0.337 0.373 0.733

.................., ..., ...

15. A square has a perimeter of 60 cm. What is the length of one of its sides? .... cm

Part B

16. Look at the prices of rides at the fair. What would it cost to go on the big wheel once and the dodgems twice? £...............

Big wheel	£1.40
Dodgems	£1.25

17. Find the missing number:
60 × [?] = 48 000 ....

18. Harry has 450 ml of custard and uses 0.2 litres. How many millilitres of custard does he have left? .... ml

19. Write out the first five multiples of 12.

.........., ..., ..., ..., ...

20. A table weighs 41.43 kg. How much does it weigh to the nearest kilogram? .... kg

21. Count forwards to work out –6 + 10. ....

22. Work out $3\frac{1}{3} \times 2$. Give your answer as a mixed number. ....

23. A textbook costs £3.72. How much do 1000 textbooks cost? £...............

24. What prime number is between 25 and 30? ....

25. A tree was planted 144 months ago. How many years ago was it planted? .... years

26. Work out 19 020 – 11 800. ....

27. What is $6\frac{5}{7} - \frac{2}{7}$? Give your answer as a mixed number. ....

28. Work out 70 ÷ 14. ....

29. Find angle K.

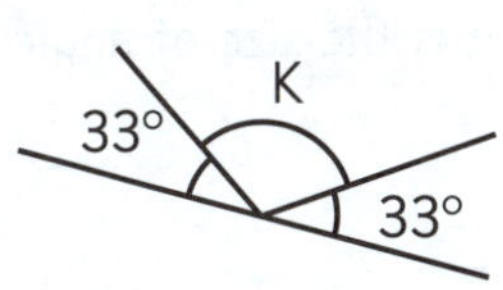

.... °

30. Marina has 104 hens. One week, each hen laid 5 eggs. How many eggs did the hens lay altogether? ....

Section 2 Progress Test

1) $\frac{65}{100}$ of the children in a school bring a packed lunch.
The rest have a school dinner.

Write the proportion that bring a packed lunch as a decimal.

1 mark

What percentage of the children in the school have a school dinner? %

1 mark

2) There are 4 houses for sale in a village.
The prices for each house are:

£556 197 £525 355 £593 785 £510 425

The most expensive house is reduced by £10 000 every month until it sells 3 months later.
How much does it sell for? £

1 mark

3) What is the area of this shape?

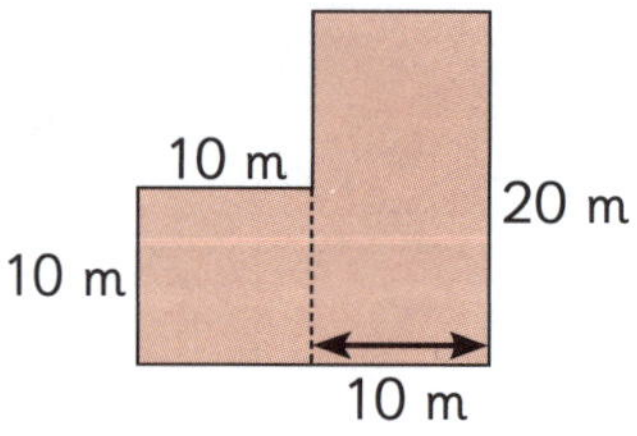

m^2

1 mark

4) Look at the numbers in the box:

8	15	20	30	80	120

Which number in the box is a common factor of 60 and 40?

1 mark

Which two numbers are multiples of 6? and

2 marks

5) What is the size of angle s?

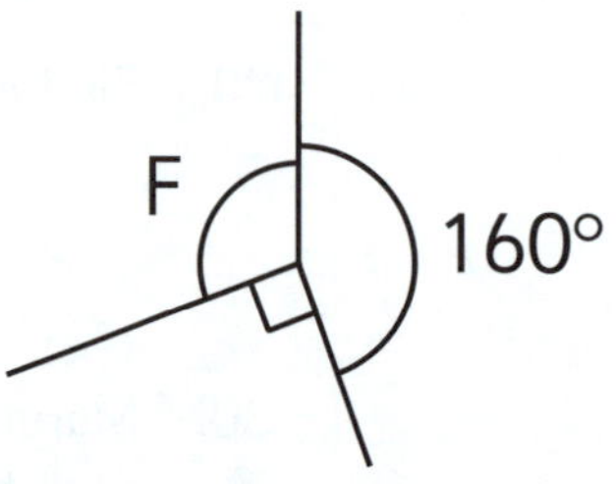

°

1 mark

Section 2 Progress Test

6) Jamal earned 123 743 points in a computer game.
Georgia earned 90 200 points.

How many points did they earn in total?

1 mark

7) The line graph shows how long it took Rani and Tony to swim a 350 m race in a lake.

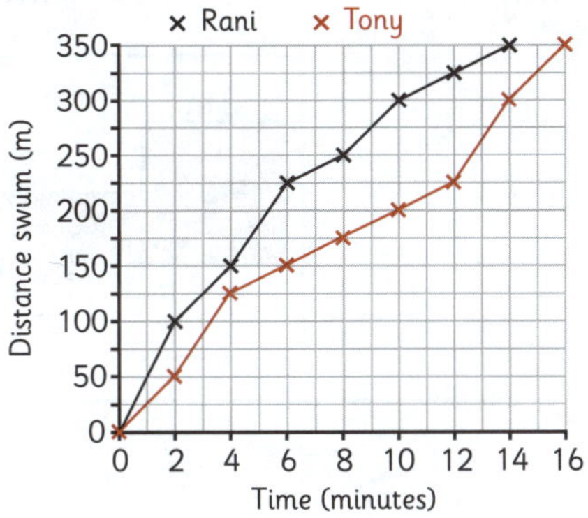

How much longer did it take Tony to swim the first 300 m of the race than Rani?

mins

1 mark

After 12 minutes, how much further had Rani swum than Tony?

m

1 mark

8) Work out this subtraction, giving your answer in millimetres.

550 mm – 35 cm = ☐ mm

1 mark

9) Each cake at a fair has been cut into 12 pieces.
There are 360 pieces in total.

How many cakes are there?

1 mark

There is enough cake for everyone at the fair to take 4 pieces with no cake left over. How many people are at the fair?

1 mark

10) Fill in the missing numbers.

$$\frac{32}{5} - \frac{25}{5} = \square\frac{\square}{5}$$

1 mark

Section 2 Listening Tests

Go to cgpbooks.co.uk/MA-Year5 or scan the QR code on the right to find the audio files for these listening tests. Listen carefully to each question before writing down your answer in the spaces provided for each test.

Each test has ten questions. You will have 5 seconds to answer each of the first five questions, and 10 seconds to answer each of the last five questions.

Section 2 Listening Tests

Listening Test 1

1. ....
2. ....
3. ....
4. ....
5. ....
6. .... %
7. ....
8. ....
9. .... m^2
10. l

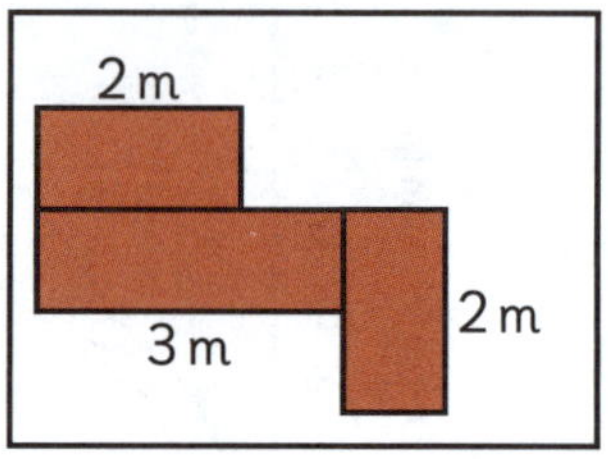

Listening Test 2

1. ....
2. ....
3. ....
4. ....
5. ....
6. .... m
7. £ ....
8. .... months
9. .... km
10. ....

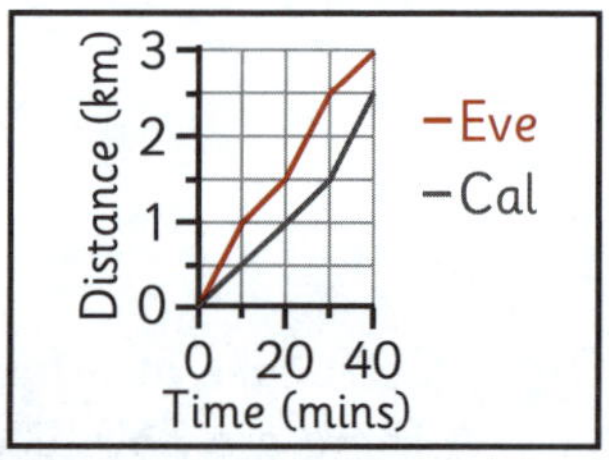

Listening Test 3

1. ....
2. ....
3. ....
4. .... °C
5. ....
6. £ ....
7. ....
8. ....
9. .... m
10. .... cm^2

5.38	5.694
5.79	5.91
5.856	4.84

Test 1

Part A

1. Which number between 50 and 70 is a cube number? ....

2. $\frac{14}{9} - \frac{?}{9} = \frac{7}{9}$
What is the missing number? ....

3. Round 84.02 to 1 decimal place. ....

4. What is the area of the shaded part of this shape?

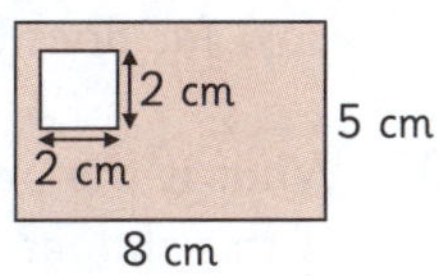

.... cm^2

5. How many factors of 35 are prime? ....

6. What is $\frac{3}{4} \times 9$? Give your answer as an improper fraction. ....

7. Enzo cycles 8227 m.
Jill cycles 3400 m less than Enzo.
How far does Jill cycle? .... m

8. What is 6.35 × 1000? ....

9. What year is represented by the Roman numeral MMXIV? ....

10. Three angles meet around a point.
Two of the angles are 130° and 150°.
What is the size of the third angle? .... °

11. Which is smaller, A: 23 feet or B: 10 m?
Use the conversion 1 metre ≈ 3 feet. ....

12. In a class, $\frac{1}{3}$ of the pupils have blonde hair. $\frac{5}{9}$ have brown hair. What fraction have neither blonde nor brown hair? ....

13. Work out 144 ÷ 24. ....

14. This line graph shows the temperature of two pans of water. How much cooler was Pan B after 3 minutes than Pan A?

.... °C

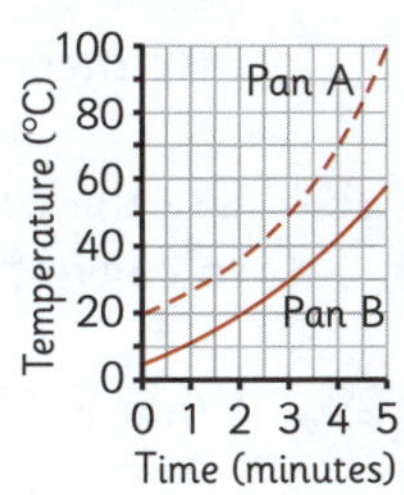

15. Alana pours two 0.83 litre bottles of cola into a jug. How much cola is there in total, in ml? .... ml

Part B

16. Estimate 7.93 × 8.1 by rounding each number to the nearest whole number. ....

17. Which is bigger: $\frac{12}{7}$ or $\frac{35}{21}$? ....

18. Point P is translated 3 units to the left and 2 units up. Which of the points on the grid shows its new position?

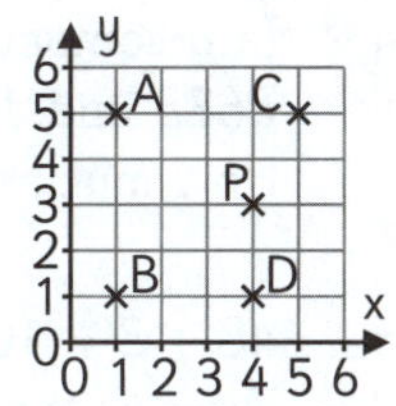

....

19. Work out the missing number:
37 512 + [?] = 77 712 ....

20. Luke thinks of a number. He adds 300 to it, then subtracts 802, and gets 425.
What number was he thinking of? ....

21. What is the area of a rectangle that is $3\frac{1}{2}$ m wide and 8 m long? .... m^2

22. Which of the amounts below is lighter than 1.06 kg?

1.075 kg	1.054 kg	1.09 kg

.... kg

23. A football weighs 410 g.
How much would 6 footballs weigh? .... g

24. $\frac{13}{20}$ of Lizzi's friends have siblings.
What percentage of her friends don't have siblings? .... %

25. What is the perimeter of this shape?

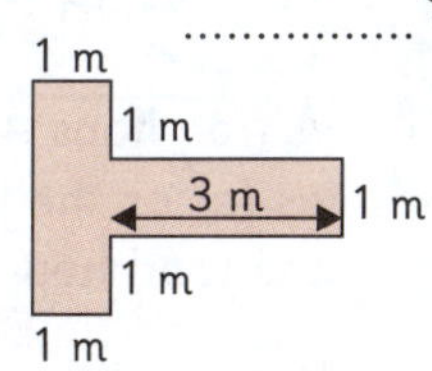

.... m

26. 12 × 17 = 6 × [?] × 17
What is the missing number? ....

27. What is 87 mm + 12.5 cm, in cm? .... cm

28. Bobby divides 2436 apples equally between three lorries. How many apples are in each lorry? ....

29. What is $4\frac{2}{9}$ as an improper fraction? ....

30. A TV weighs 11.1 kg. A computer weighs 8600 g. How much do they weigh in total, in kg? .... kg

Test 2

Part A

1. Work out 5.23 × 10. ....

2. Round 16.83 to the nearest tenth. ....

3. What is 83 904 – 5000? ....

4. In a competition, Helen wins £683 and Jamila wins £345. How much do they win in total? £..............

5. 48 ÷ 3 = 10 + [?]
What is the missing number? ....

6. What is $7^2 - 3^3$? ....

7. Gareth has $\frac{3}{4}$ of a litre of squash.
He drinks $\frac{7}{20}$ of a litre of it.
How much is left as a fraction? l

8. In a diving competition, Tia scored 233.85 and Steph scored 232.75. What is the difference between their scores? ....

9. This line graph shows the distance travelled by a remote controlled car. How far did it travel between 10 seconds and 25 seconds? .... m

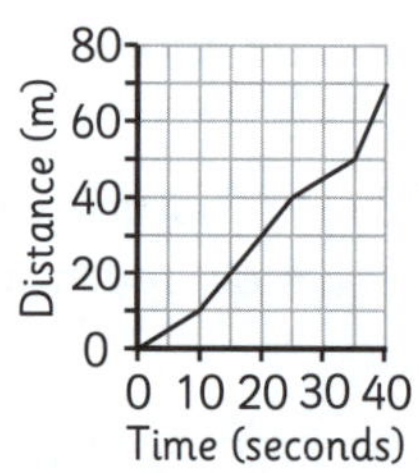

10. What is $\frac{11}{15} + \frac{1}{5}$? ....

11. A frog hops 4 m. A toad hops 20% as far as the frog. How far does the toad hop in cm? .... cm

12. 12 friends eat $\frac{5}{6}$ of a pizza each.
How many pizzas do they eat in total? ....

13. 74 000 pebbles, to the nearest thousand, are found on a beach. What is the largest possible number of pebbles? ....

14. How many different factors of 32 are prime? ....

15. $7\frac{1}{2} = \frac{?}{2}$
What is the missing number? ....

Part B

16. A cap costs £3.70. A T-shirt costs £4.10 more than a cap. What is the total cost of a cap and a T-shirt? £...............

17. Which is the smallest: $\frac{2}{3}$, $\frac{8}{9}$ or $\frac{15}{18}$? ....

18. Poppy runs 2150 m. Stan runs four times as far as Poppy. How far does Stan run? .... m

19. What is the perimeter of this shape? .... m

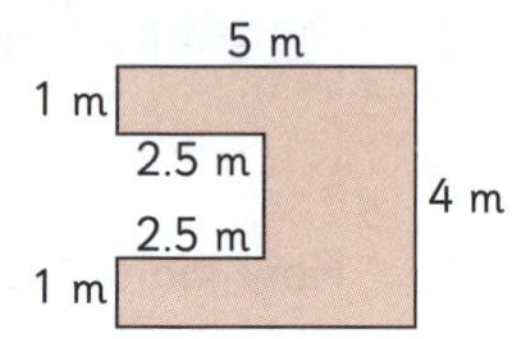

20. Hassan was born in MMVII. His grandma was born 65 years earlier. In what year was his grandma born, in numbers? ....

21. What is 296 ÷ 8? ....

22. Kyle has 100 plants in his greenhouse. $\frac{11}{20}$ are tomatoes and the rest are lettuces. How many lettuces are in the greenhouse? ....

23. What is the size of angle x? .... °

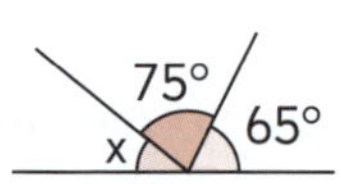

24. A rectangle has a length of 12 cm. The area of this rectangle is 36 cm^2. What is the width of the rectangle? .... cm

25. How many prime numbers are smaller than 5? ....

26. What is the area of this shape? .... m^2

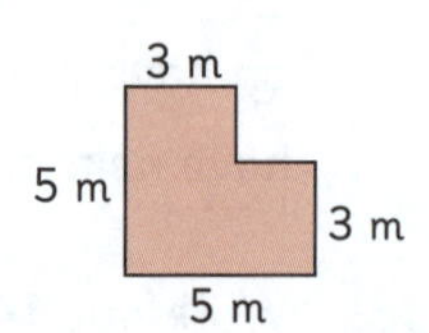

27. A company washes 12 cars per hour. How long would it take them to wash 252 cars? .... hours

28. Use the conversion 100 g ≈ 4 ounces to convert 36 ounces into grams. .... g

29. What is 1.5 litres + 8100 ml, in litres? l

30. A bakery makes 338 muffins. They sell 112 muffins on Monday and 95 on Tuesday. How many are left? ....

Test 3

Warm Up Questions

1) Which of the fractions in the box on the right are smaller than 0.5?

2) Which of the fractions in the box on the right is bigger than 0.75?

$\frac{7}{8}$ $\frac{5}{16}$ $\frac{3}{4}$ $\frac{13}{24}$ $\frac{5}{12}$

Part A

1. Round £96.29 to the nearest whole pound. £..................

2. Which is smaller: 1087 g or 1.87 kg? ....

3. What is 11^2? ....

4. What is the missing number?
24 561 + [?] = 31 561 ....

5. A jug holds 2420 ml of water and a bucket holds 7.5 litres. How much more does the bucket hold than the jug, in ml? .... ml

6. This line graph shows the heights of two sunflowers, A and B. How much more did Sunflower B grow between day 9 and day 15 than Sunflower A? .... cm

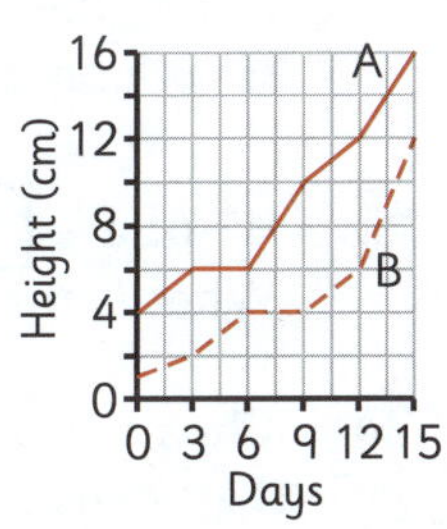

7. What year is represented by the Roman numeral MCMLII? ....

8. Work out 83 × 9. ....

9. Sam has 4.3 ml of eye drops left. Each drop is 0.2 ml. How much will be left after he uses 3 drops? .... ml

10. Two flower pots contain 8.7 kg of soil in total. One contains 3900 g. How much soil is in the other flower pot, in grams? .... g

11. What is $\frac{13}{7}$ as a mixed number? ....

12. Lyndsey has 50 pairs of socks. 35 pairs are spotty and the rest are plain. What percentage of the pairs of socks are plain? .... %

Part B

13. The perimeter of a square is 36 m. What is the area of the square? .... m^2

14. Which of the numbers below is a composite number?

17	29	43	61	63

....

15. What is the size of angle A? .... °

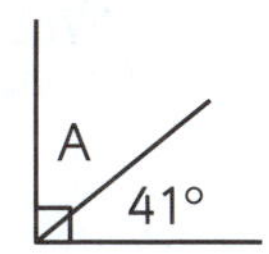

16. What is $2 + \frac{7}{4}$ as a mixed number? ....

17. Amira paid £350 for three nights at a hotel. The first night cost £118 and the second night cost £130. How much did the third night cost? £................

18. Use the conversion 5 cm ≈ 2 inches to convert 40 cm into inches. .... inches

19. Work out 137 ÷ 1000. ....

20. This shape is made out of two identical rectangles. What is its perimeter? .... cm

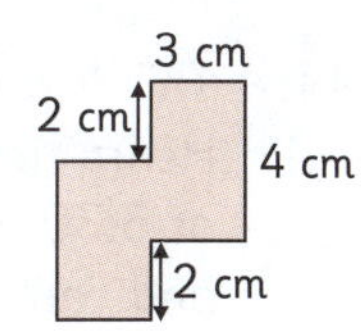

21. 84 ÷ 4 = [?] × 7
What is the missing number? ....

22. Damian drinks $3\frac{2}{3}$ bottles of water every day. How many bottles will he drink in 7 days, as a mixed number? ....

23. How many sweets would be needed to fill 120 bags with 30 sweets each? ....

24. Which fraction below is the biggest?

$\frac{5}{8}$	$\frac{1}{2}$	$\frac{17}{24}$

....

Test 4

Part A

1. How many ml are there in 6.07 litres? .... ml

2. How many prime factors does 42 have? ....

3. What is 18.27 kg rounded to the nearest kilogram? .... kg

4. What is $\frac{2}{3} - \frac{7}{12}$? ....

5. A regular skipping rope is 132 cm long. A giant skipping rope is 3 times as long. How long is a giant skipping rope? .... cm

6. What is the perimeter of this shape?

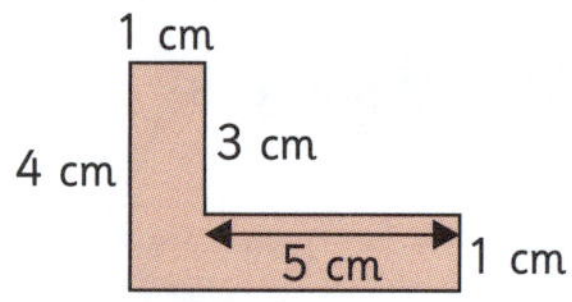

.... cm

7. What is nineteen sixths as a mixed number? ....

8. A desert is 35 °C. A mountain top is 39 °C colder than the desert. What is the temperature on the mountain top? .... °C

9. What is 30.8 ÷ 100? ....

10. Which number below is not a square number?

16	27	36	49	64

....

11. This is a bus timetable. Henry gets to the beach at 6:30 pm. If he waits and catches the next bus, how long will it be until he gets to town? .... mins

Harbour	Beach	Town
18:15	18:29	18:45
19:10	19:24	19:40
20:05	20:19	20:35

12. Arnie buys 11 pints of milk. How many litres of milk does he buy? Use the conversion 1 litre ≈ 2 pints. l

13. What is 10 750 + 4200? ....

14. Iona has three-quarters of a circular pie. She eats a slice measuring 40°. How many degrees of the pie is left? .... °

15. Work out $1\frac{2}{7} \times 4$, giving your answer as a mixed number. ....

Part B

16. Nadya has 1 m of string. She uses 43% to tie up a parcel and 0.4 m to hang a picture frame. How many metres of string does she have left? .... m

17. What is 9523 + 2400 – 375? ....

18. A rectangle is 6 cm wide and has an area of 72 cm^2. What is its length? .... cm

19. 8 identical party hats cost £25.60 in total. How much does each hat cost? £..............

20. Point W is reflected in the mirror line. What are its new coordinates?

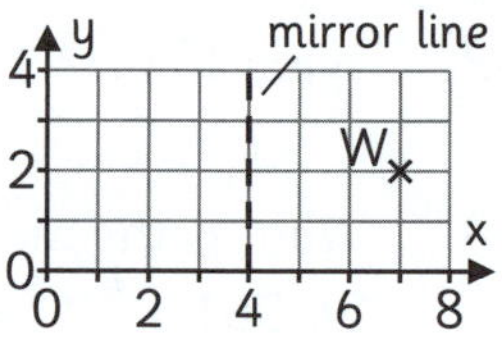

....

21. What is $\frac{7}{8} + \frac{5}{8}$ as a mixed number? ....

22. A plumber has 4.6 m of pipe. She cuts off 0.4 m, then divides the rest of the pipe into 6 equal pieces. How long is each piece of pipe, in cm? .... cm

23. 91 651 – [?] = 88 651
What is the missing number? ....

24. Chris has an apple with his lunch for 149 days in a row. How long is this in weeks and days?

.... weeks .... days

25. A battery weighs 28 g to the nearest gram. What is the lightest the battery could be to one decimal place? .... g

26. Write 2025 as a Roman numeral. ....

27. Aki knits $\frac{3}{10}$ of a scarf on Sunday, $\frac{7}{20}$ of it on Monday and $\frac{13}{40}$ of it on Tuesday. On which day did she knit the most? ....

28. What is 76 × 5? ....

29. What is the area of this shape?

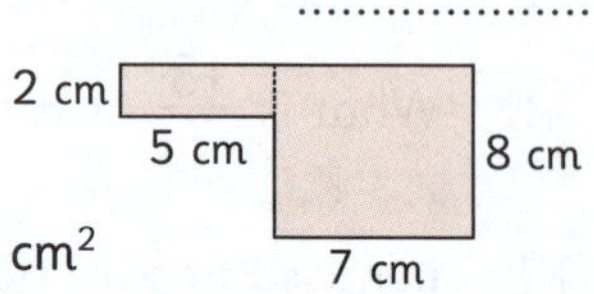

.... cm^2

30. 150 ÷ [?] = 5 × 5
What is the missing number? ....

Test 5

Part A

1. Write the value of the 1 in 9.314 in words.

2. Which is smallest: $\frac{9}{16}$, $\frac{3}{8}$ or $\frac{5}{8}$?

3. What is 1200 × 30?

4. The graph shows the volume of water in a tank. How much water was used between Tuesday and Thursday? l

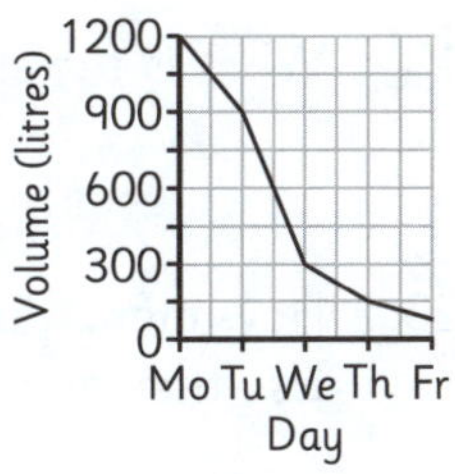

5. How many times bigger than 8.29 is 8290?

6. The temperature inside a huddle of penguins is 21 °C. Outside the huddle it is –45 °C. How much warmer is it inside? .... °C

7. 46 635 + ? = 76 635
What is the missing number?

8. What is $2\frac{5}{7}$ as an improper fraction?

9. Rohit thinks of a number. He subtracts 104 from it, then adds 423 to get 650. What number was he thinking of?

10. Vera bought a necklace and two identical rings for £16. The necklace cost £9. How much did one ring cost? £...............

11. What is 5.5 kg + 3500 g, in kg? .... kg

12. What is the perimeter of this shape? .... cm

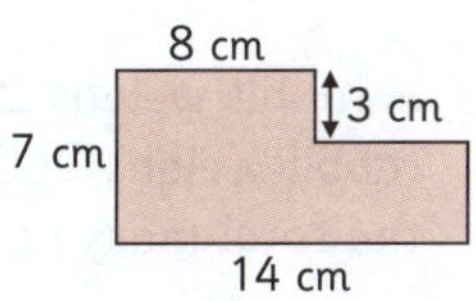

13. What is 88 000 ÷ 110?

14. Which is larger: 100 cm or 36 inches?
Use the conversion 5 cm ≈ 2 inches.

15. What year is represented by the Roman numeral MDCCCV?

Part B

16. Round 47.85 to 1 decimal place.

17. Which of these weights is the biggest:
25 700 g, 2.6 kg or 26.6 kg?

18. Work out $\frac{3}{8} + \frac{9}{16}$.

19. The area of this rectangle is 48 cm². What is the missing length? .... cm

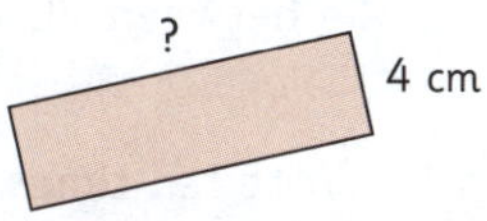

20. Which of the numbers below is a composite number?

2	3	5	7	9

21. Pam ran 4300 m. She dropped her keys after 1.2 km. How far back did she have to run to find her keys, in m? .... m

22. What is $3^2 + 4^2$?

23. Three angles meet to make one whole turn. Two of the angles are 65° and 125°. What is the size of the third angle? ....°

24. Naveen's rose bush is 60 cm tall. His sunflower is $1\frac{4}{5}$ as tall as his rose bush. How tall is his sunflower? .... cm

25. 13 × 64 = 13 × ? × 4
What is the missing number?

26. Mo earns £12.25 an hour. How much will he earn if he works a total of 20 hours? £...............

27. Work out 7404 – 1300.

28. $\frac{12}{25}$ of the members of an athletics club are runners. What percentage of the club's members are not runners? .... %

29. What is $3 - \frac{7}{10}$ as a mixed number?

30. Posy has 156 lollipops. She wants to share them equally between 12 people. How many will each person have?

Test 6

Part A

1. Which of these lengths is the shortest: 10 000 mm, 1000 cm or 1 m? ....

2. What is 27.17 to the nearest tenth? ....

3. Work out 16 320 + 2000 + 300. ....

4. Which two prime numbers lie between 20 and 30? .... and ....

5. Write ten times $\frac{2}{7}$ as a mixed number. ....

6. There are 300 000 litres of water in a pond, to the nearest 100 000 litres. Which value in the box could be the exact number of litres?

238 452	351 561	308 579

....

7. Ami colours in $\frac{2}{5}$ of a picture in week 1, $\frac{6}{20}$ in week 2, and $\frac{3}{10}$ in week 3. In which week did she colour the most? ....

8. 139 452 + [?] = 155 452
What is the missing number? ....

9. What is the total area of this shape?

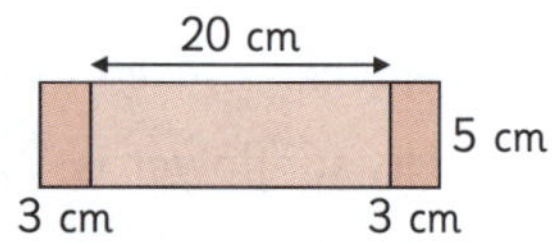

.... cm^2

10. Eli makes ice cubes from a 330 ml can of cola. He uses 25 ml per cube. How much cola will he have left if he makes 8 ice cubes? .... ml

11. Work out $5^2 + 9^2$. ....

12. Write 2017 as a Roman numeral. ....

13. The graph shows the temperatures of two ovens after they're turned on. How much hotter was Oven A than Oven B at 30 seconds?

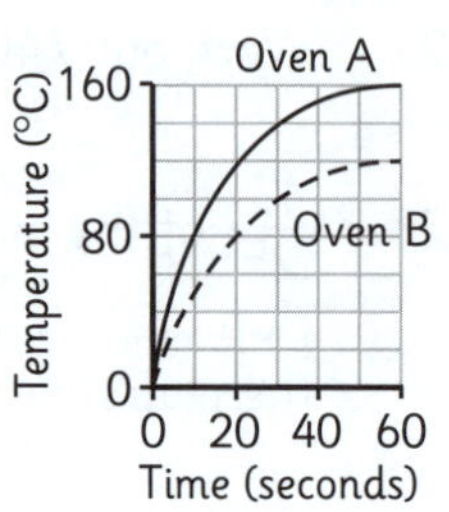

.... °C

14. What is 84 ÷ 14? ....

15. $\frac{30}{8} - \frac{9}{4} = \frac{?}{2}$
What is the missing number? ....

Part B

16. [?] ÷ 100 = 0.93
What is the missing number? ....

17. Work out 13 531 – 2000. ....

18. What is $\frac{5}{6} + \frac{1}{2}$ as a mixed number? ....

19. What is the size of angle B?

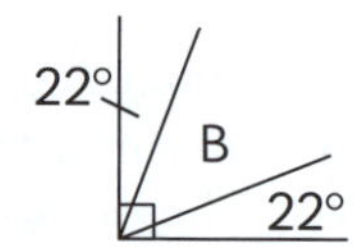

.... °

20. How many pints are in 2000 ml? Use the conversion 1 litre ≈ 2 pints. .... pints

21. Avril has 25 nuts. 11 are almonds, 9 are walnuts and the rest are pecans. What percentage are pecans? .... %

22. Which number below is not a cube number?

8	27	64	81	125

....

23. 5 hats and 2 scarves cost £34. One scarf costs £4.50. What is the cost of one hat? £.................

24. A drawing pin has a length of 1.893 mm. Another pin has a length of 1.89 mm. What is the difference in their lengths? .... mm

25. Which is the smallest: $\frac{19}{24}$, $\frac{7}{12}$ or $\frac{5}{6}$? ....

26. What is the perimeter of this shape?

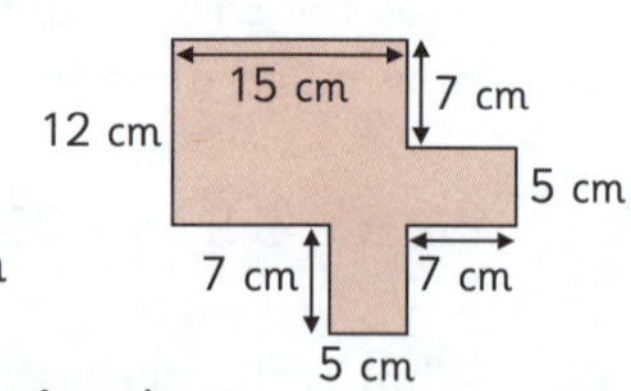

.... cm

27. A rabbit weighs 2300 g. Another rabbit weighs 2600 g. What is the total mass of the rabbits, in kg? .... kg

28. What is 67 × 8? ....

29. Estimate 3.55 + 2.29 by rounding each number to one decimal place. ....

30. Luna has 2 litres of soup. She eats 20% of it. How much soup is left over, in ml? .... ml

Test 7

Warm Up Questions

Look at the shape on the right.

1) What is the length of side X?

2) What is the length of side Y?

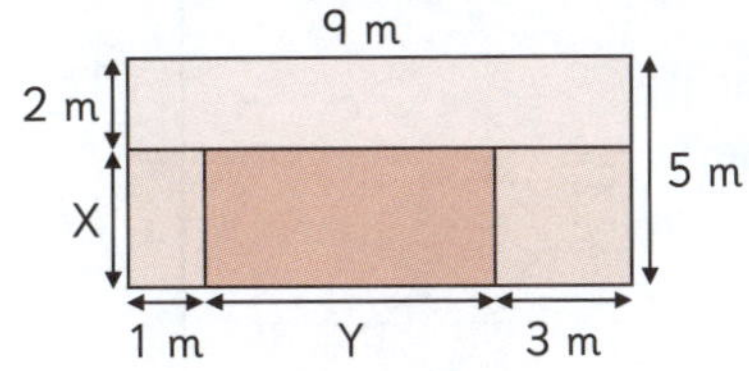

Part A

1. Write the value of the 7 in 3.097 in words. ....

2. Write down the square numbers between 5 and 20. .... and ....

3. What is the missing number? $\frac{2}{5} + \frac{3}{10} = \frac{?}{10}$ ....

4. In Roman numerals, a film was made in the year MCMLXXXVII. What year is this in numbers? ....

5. The point A is reflected in the mirror line. What are its new coordinates? ....

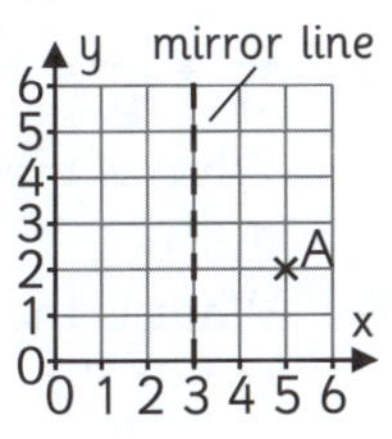

6. A tower of cans is 0.6 m tall. There are 5 cans in the tower. How tall is each can, in cm? .... cm

7. Work out 16 723 + 2100. ....

8. Three angles form a straight line. Two of the angles are 34° and 48°. What is the size of the third angle? .... °

9. Work out $\frac{7}{10} - \frac{21}{100}$. ....

10. Erin has a 1.25 litre carton of juice. She drinks 275 ml of it. How many ml of juice does she have left? .... ml

11. What is 5600 ÷ 70? ....

12. A small pot can hold $\frac{3}{8}$ of a bag of pasta. As a mixed number, how many bags of pasta can 10 small pots hold? ....

Part B

13. Which is biggest: $\frac{5}{10}$, $\frac{31}{50}$ or $\frac{63}{100}$? ....

14. A smartphone costs £299.49. How much is this to the nearest pound? £..........

15. The graph shows the distance of a kite from the ground. How far did the kite fall between 5 and 10 seconds? .... m

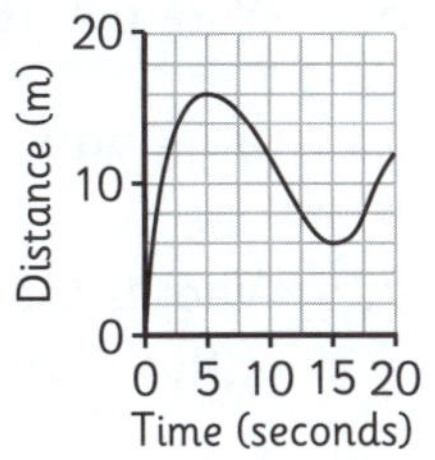

16. How many times smaller than 658.2 is 65.82? ....

17. Meng has some coloured pencils. 20% are green. What fraction of the pencils are not green? ....

18. 67 732 – [?] = 67 662
What is the missing number? ....

19. How many ounces are in 700 g? Use the conversion 100 g ≈ 4 ounces. .... oz

20. What is $3\frac{5}{6}$ as an improper fraction? ....

21. What is 80 × 900? ....

22. To the nearest thousand, there are 510 000 grains of sand in a timer. What is the smallest possible number of grains of sand? ....

23. How many different factors of 56 are prime? ....

24. What is the area of this shape? .... cm^2

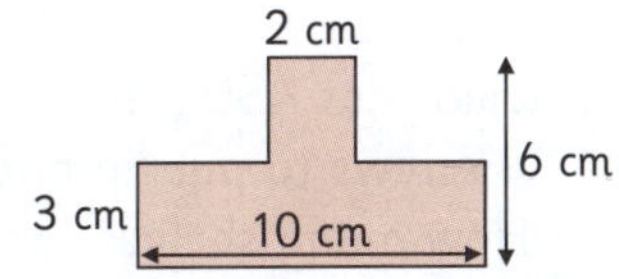

Test 8

Part A

1. Lukas drives 8.56 km. How far is this rounded to 1 decimal place? .... km

2. What is 180 ÷ 60? ....

3. Which of these lengths is the shortest: 4461 mm, 44.61 cm or 4.461 m? ....

4. Three friends each have a small pizza. Leo eats $\frac{15}{18}$ of his, Jen eats $\frac{7}{9}$ of hers, and Andy eats $\frac{2}{3}$ of his. Who has the most left? ....

5. Work out 18 458 + 4800. ....

6. Write 992 as a Roman numeral. ....

7. What is the area of this shape? .... m^2

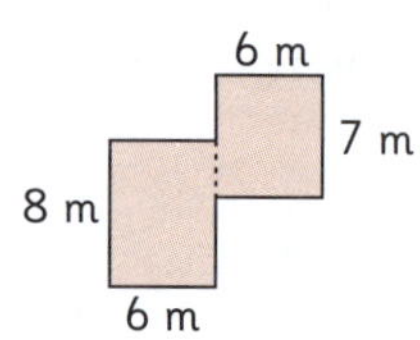

8. Two scooters weigh 5.5 kg in total. The lighter scooter weighs 2500 g. How much does the heavier scooter weigh, in grams? .... g

9. 7.628 × [?] = 762.8
   What is the missing number? ....

10. What is $\frac{7}{9} - \frac{2}{3}$? ....

11. Eni sells bracelets for £25 each. The graph shows her monthly sales. How many bracelets did she sell in June? ....

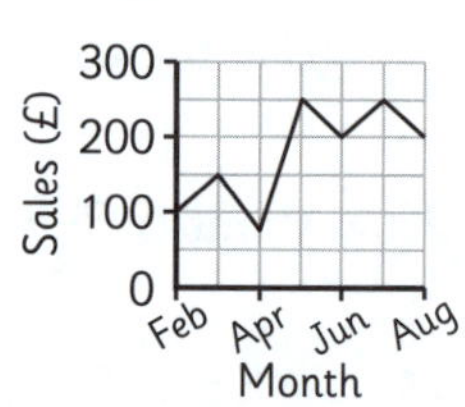

12. What is 49 × 4? ....

13. Estimate 14.74 – 6.55 by rounding each number to the nearest whole number. ....

14. How many prime numbers are there between 40 and 45? ....

15. Elliot has 450 screws. He needs 4 screws to put up one shelf. How many shelves can he put up? ....

Part B

16. Write 1.07 as a mixed number. ....

17. Which is smaller, A: 230 kg or B: 450 pounds? 1 kg ≈ 2 pounds. ....

18. The temperature inside a house is 23 °C. Outside the house it is 25 °C colder. What is the temperature outside? .... °C

19. Work out $4^3 - 2^3$. ....

20. To the nearest ml, there is 14 ml of medicine on a spoon. What is the most medicine that could be on the spoon to one decimal place? .... ml

21. What is $2\frac{2}{5} \times 9$? Give your answer as an improper fraction. ....

22. What is the size of angle E? .... °

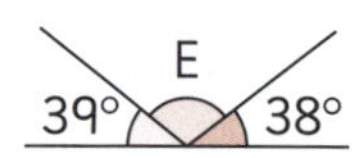

23. $\frac{5}{3} + \frac{?}{6} = \frac{13}{3}$
    What is the missing number? ....

24. What is the perimeter of this shape? .... cm

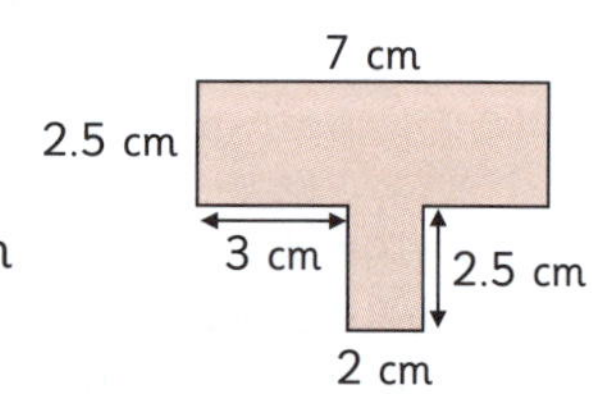

25. 59 440 – [?] = 39 440
    What is the missing number? ....

26. What is 8.9 litres – 6750 ml, in ml? .... ml

27. Gabs can read $1\frac{1}{5}$ pages of a book per minute. How many pages can she read in one hour? ....

28. Which of the numbers below is a composite number?

73	79	83	89	93

....

29. Helen has 1 litre of milk. She uses 30% of it to make pancakes, then drinks 250 ml. How much does she have left in ml? .... ml

30. How many seeds are needed to fill 48 packets with 6 seeds each? ....

Test 9

Part A

1. Round £89.95 to the nearest pound. £..................

2. What is 22 430 + 16 000? ....

3. Which symbol (=, < or >) should go in the box?
204 ÷ 1000 [?] 0.204 × 10 ....

4. Which is smaller: $\frac{4}{15}$ or $\frac{7}{30}$? ....

5. The point B is reflected in the mirror line. What are its new coordinates? ....

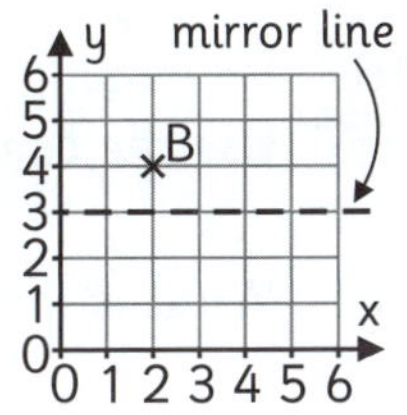

6. How many different factors of 66 are prime? ....

7. Three angles meet around a point. Two of the angles are 140° and 82°. What is the size of the third angle? ....°

8. What is 10^3? ....

9. Which of the weights below is lighter than 2.108 kg?

2150 g	2099 g	2200 g

.... g

10. What is the area of the shaded part of this shape? .... m^2

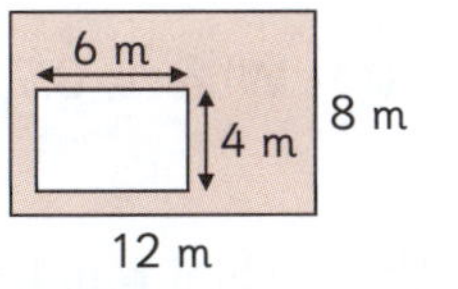

11. A dog weighs 5 kg. A kitten weighs 20% as much as the dog. How much does the kitten weigh, in grams? .... g

12. What is $1\frac{1}{3} \times 5$? Give your answer as an improper fraction. ....

13. Work out 774 ÷ 6. ....

14. $\frac{18}{25}$ of Wasima's books are non-fiction. What percentage of Wasima's books are fiction? .... %

15. What is 2.6 litres + 450 ml in litres? l

Part B

16. How many pints are in 152 litres? Use the conversion 1 litre ≈ 2 pints. .... pints

17. $1\frac{9}{10} - \frac{?}{5} = 1\frac{3}{10}$
What is the missing number? ....

18. A company has £493 055 in savings. They save an extra £100 each month. How much do they have after 9 months? £....................

19. What is 590 × 8? ....

20. This rectangle has a perimeter of 38 cm. What is the difference between its length and its width? .... cm

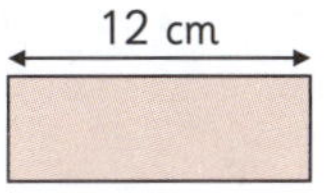

21. What year is represented by the Roman numeral MCMXLV? ....

22. How many booklets would be needed to fill 500 boxes with 40 booklets each? ....

23. Write $\frac{7}{14} + \frac{5}{7}$ as a mixed number. ....

24. Work out the missing number:
24 641 − [?] = 7641 ....

25. Tahel shares 511 screws equally between 7 containers. How many screws are in each container? ....

26. The graph shows the distance Kieron cycled on his bike ride. How far did he cycle between 8:00 and 9:00? .... km

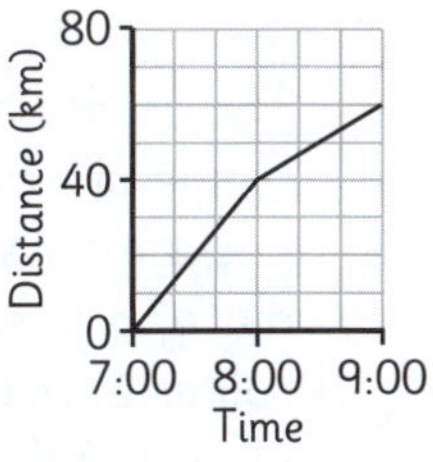

27. Which of these lengths is the longest: 7.405 m, 7.54 m or 7.450 m? .... m

28. In a class, $\frac{2}{5}$ of the pupils like tea, $\frac{3}{10}$ dislike tea, and the rest are undecided. What fraction are undecided? ....

29. What is 690.6 ÷ 100? ....

30. Andy thinks of a number. He subtracts 209, then adds 297 and gets 888. What number was he thinking of? ....

Test 10

Warm Up Questions

1) Find all of the square numbers in the box on the right.
2) Find all of the cube numbers in the box on the right.

9 12 56 64
81 125 216

Part A

1. Which symbol (< or >) should go in the box? 5.402 [?] 5.408 ....

2. Which is larger: $\frac{13}{32}$ or $\frac{3}{8}$? ....

3. Write 1066 as a Roman numeral. ....

4. Which two prime numbers are between 50 and 60? .... and ....

5. Work out the missing number: 43 572 + [?] = 73 972 ....

6. The perimeter of the rectangle is equal to the perimeter of the square. What is the missing side length?

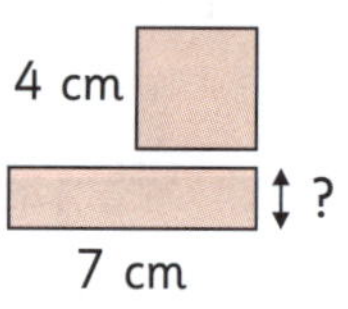

.... cm

7. What is 63 × 9? ....

8. What is $4\frac{1}{6} - 3\frac{2}{3}$? ....

9. The graph shows the temperatures of two ice packs after they are taken out of a freezer. How much colder is pack A than pack B after 3 minutes?

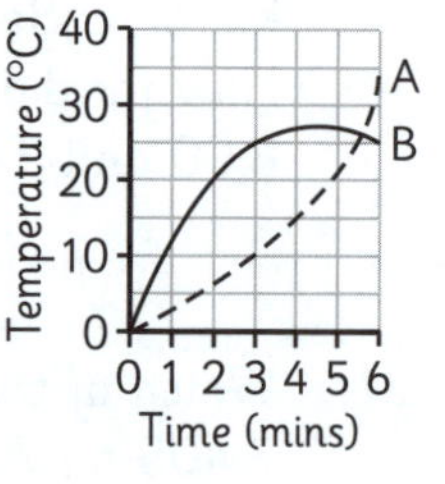

.... °C

10. What is 41 ÷ 1000? ....

11. A medium drink is 60 ml more than a small drink and 80 ml less than a large drink. A large drink is 450 ml. What is the volume of a small drink? .... ml

12. Write $6\frac{3}{4}$ as an improper fraction. ....

Part B

13. Round 62.98 to 1 decimal place. ....

14. What is 38 193 – 20 200? ....

15. How many grams are in 84 ounces? Use the conversion 100 g ≈ 4 ounces. .... g

16. What is the size of angle C? .... °

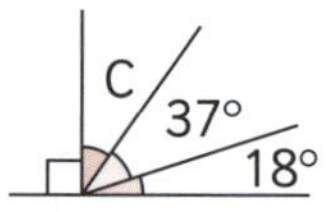

17. There are 604 500 people, to the nearest 100, living on an island. What is the smallest possible number of people living on the island? ....

18. $\frac{2}{9} + \frac{?}{27} = \frac{11}{27}$
What is the missing number? ....

19. A plant grows 0.95 cm on Monday and another 0.95 cm on Tuesday. How much taller is it now, in mm? .... mm

20. What is 0.708 × 1000? ....

21. Mani ran $1\frac{4}{5}$ km on both days of the weekend. How far did he run in total? Give your answer as a decimal. .... km

22. What is the area of this shape?

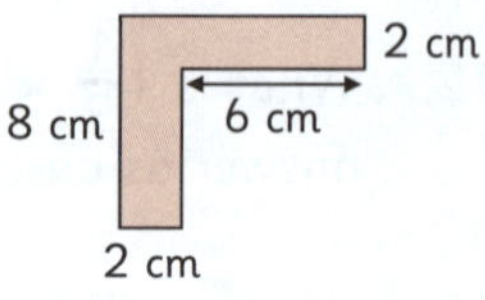

.... cm^2

23. Work out 912 ÷ 8. ....

24. Gwen has one bag containing $\frac{7}{8}$ kg of rice and another bag containing $\frac{3}{8}$ kg. How much rice does she have in total? Give your answer as a mixed number. .... kg

Test 11

Part A

1. Which of these weights is the heaviest: 3.48 kg, 3.477 kg or 3.472 kg? .... kg

2. $\frac{4}{5}$ of the players on a football team are right-footed. What percentage of the players are left-footed? .... %

3. Which is longer, A: 16 inches or B: 35 cm? Use the conversion 5 cm ≈ 2 inches. ....

4. Round 5.26 to the nearest whole number. ....

5. In a charity walk, Leon is sponsored £4.25 for every 1 km he walks. How much does he raise if he walks 20 km? £....................

6. What is $9^2 - 8^2$? ....

7. What is the perimeter of this shape?

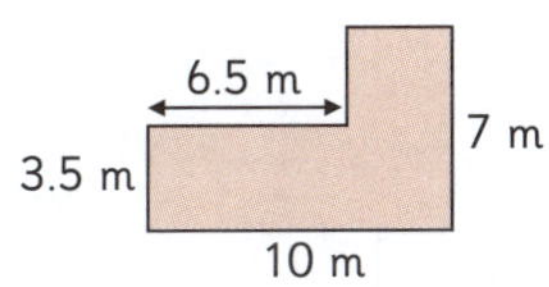

.... m

8. What year is represented by the Roman numeral MCMXCVIII? ....

9. $2\frac{11}{12} + \frac{?}{12} = 3\frac{5}{12}$
What is the missing number? ....

10. Keima shares 720 ml of soup equally between 3 bowls. How much soup is in each bowl? .... ml

11. What is the size of angle D?

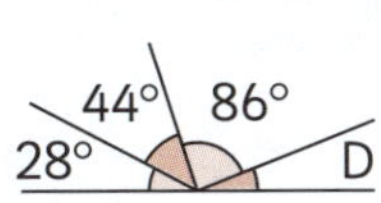

.... °

12. Mary is 121.5 cm tall. Ellie is 119.5 cm tall. How much taller than Ellie is Mary? .... cm

13. What is 28 × 7? ....

14. A grocer sells $\frac{8}{10}$ of their bananas, $\frac{3}{5}$ of their apples and $\frac{12}{20}$ of their pears. Which fruit did they sell the biggest fraction of? ....

15. What is 6.4 kg + 2600 g, in kg? .... kg

Part B

16. Which symbol (=, < or >) should go in the box?
0.334 × 100 [?] 334 ÷ 100 ....

17. What is $3 + \frac{5}{2}$ as a mixed number? ....

18. A factory has 25 412 jelly beans. It makes 10 000 more each hour for the next 8 hours. How many does it have now? ....

19. Work out 485 ÷ 5. ....

20. Which of the numbers below is a composite number?

31	37	39	41

....

21. Estimate 32.51 – 20.04 by rounding each number to one decimal place. ....

22. $1\frac{?}{8} - \frac{1}{4} = 1\frac{1}{8}$
What is the missing number? ....

23. What is 120 000 + 37 000? ....

24. The graph shows the speed of a river during a rainstorm. How much faster was the river at 24 mins than at 12 mins?

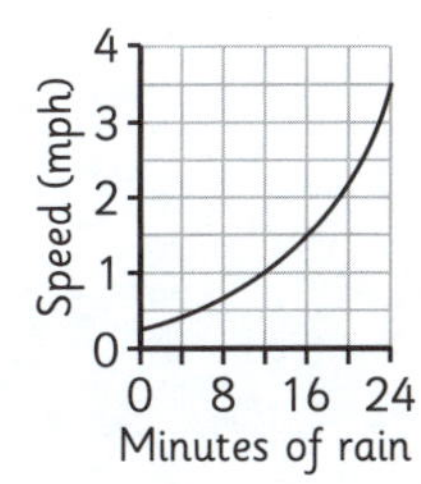

.... mph

25. Which is smaller, A: 40% of 80 or B: $\frac{3}{5}$ of 75? ....

26. Work out 47 240 – 40 060. ....

27. What is $2\frac{3}{7} \times 3$? Give your answer as an improper fraction. ....

28. 30 × 50 × [?] = 45 000
What number is missing? ....

29. This shape is made from three identical rectangles. What is the total area?

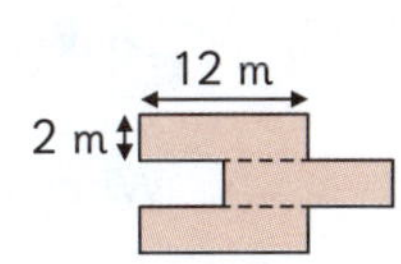

.... m^2

30. Jim has a piece of ribbon. He cuts two 15 cm pieces off and has 90 cm left. What was the original length of the ribbon, in m? .... m

Section 3 Progress Test

1) A sack of potatoes weighs 12.84 kg.

How much does it weigh to the nearest whole number? [ ] kg

1 mark

How much does it weigh to one decimal place? [ ] kg

1 mark

2) Julius writes the year MMLXVII in Roman numerals.

What year has he written? [ ]

1 mark

3) Complete the calculations below.

762 319 + 20 505 = [ ]

1 mark

67 651 + [ ] = 73 651

1 mark

4) In a class, $\frac{1}{4}$ of pupils have no siblings and $\frac{3}{8}$ have one sibling.

What fraction of pupils have more than one sibling? [ ]

1 mark

5) Look at the diagram on the right.

What is the size of angle a? [ ] °

1 mark

What is the value of x? [ ] cm

1 mark

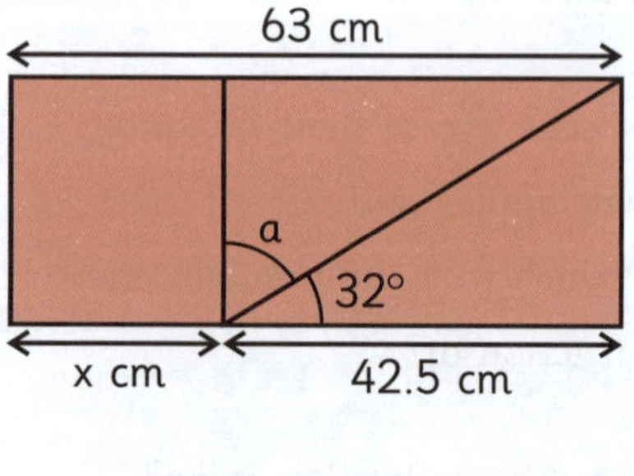

Section 3 Progress Test

6) Complete the calculations below.

$72 \times 8 =$ [ ] $255 \div 5 =$ [ ]

2 marks

7) Work out $\frac{3}{5} + \frac{4}{5}$.

Write your answer as a mixed number.

1 mark

8) Look at the shape on the right.

What is the area of the shape? [ ] m^2

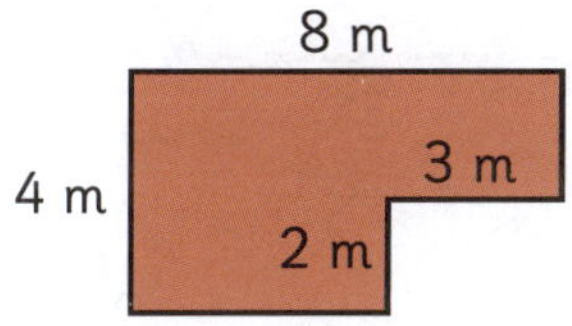

1 mark

What is the perimeter of the shape? [ ] m

1 mark

9) Salma thinks of a number. She subtracts 70, then divides by 3, and gets 310.

What number was she thinking of?

1 mark

10) The line graph shows the temperature outside Lily's office over a day.

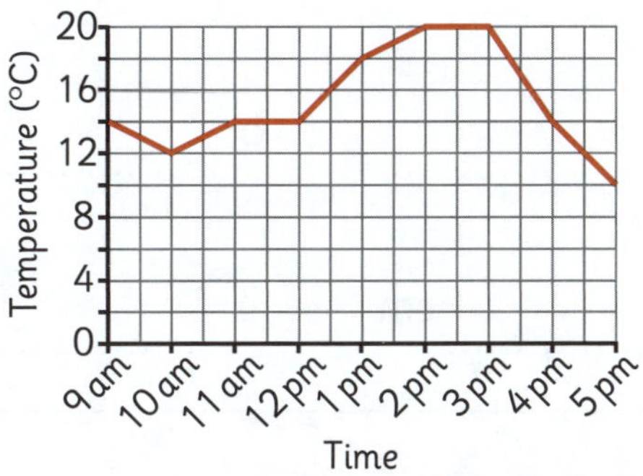

At what time was a temperature of 16 °C first recorded?

1 mark

At 5 pm, it was 8 °C warmer inside Lily's office than outside. What was the temperature inside her office? [ ] °C

1 mark

Section 3 Listening Tests

Go to cgpbooks.co.uk/MA-Year5 or scan the QR code on the right to find the audio files for these listening tests. Listen carefully to each question before writing down your answer in the spaces provided for each test.

Each test has ten questions. You will have 5 seconds to answer each of the first five questions, and 10 seconds to answer each of the last five questions.

Section 3 Listening Tests

Listening Test 1

1. ....
2. ....
3. ....
4. ....
5. ....
6. ....
7. ....
8. .... mph
9. .... m
10. ....

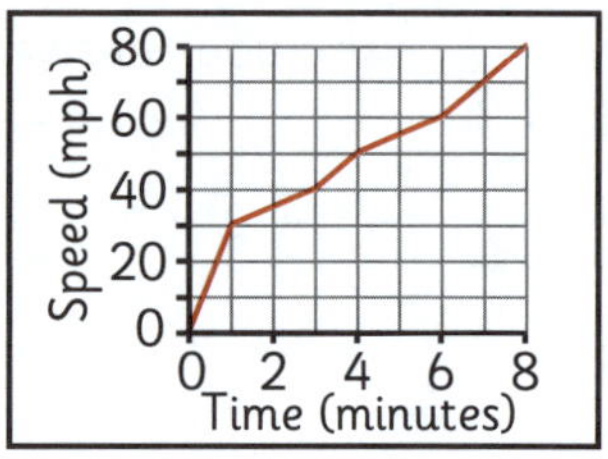

Listening Test 2

1. ....
2. ....
3. ....
4. .... oz
5. ....
6. £ ....
7. .... g
8. .... cm^2
9. ....
10. ....

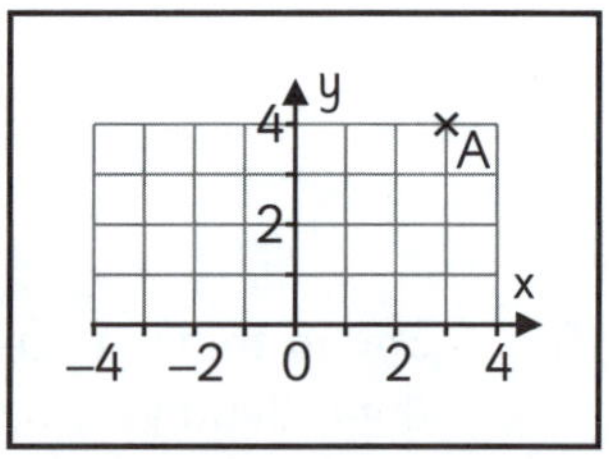

Listening Test 3

1. ....
2. ....
3. ....
4. ....
5. ....
6. .... %
7. .... °
8. .... cm
9. ....
10. .... cm

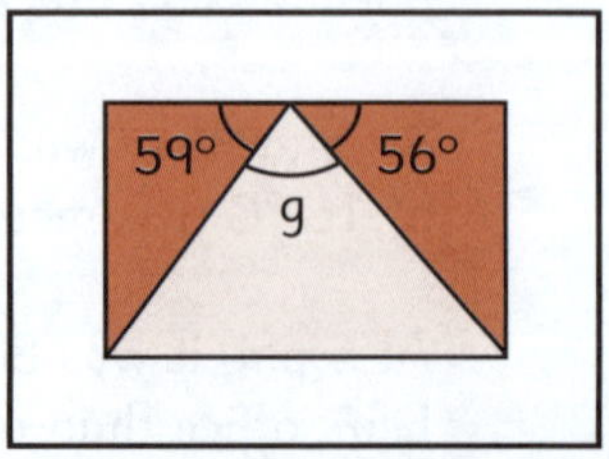

M5AQ21